A
MINDFULNESS
Guide for
SURVIVAL

RUBY WAX

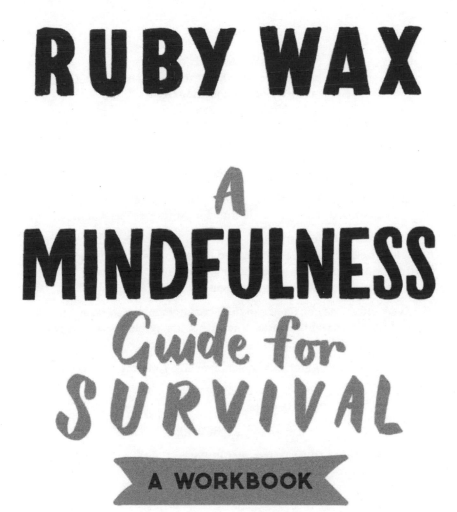

A MINDFULNESS Guide for SURVIVAL

A WORKBOOK

W

WELBECK

Published by Welbeck
An imprint of Welbeck Non-Fiction Limited,
part of Welbeck Publishing Group.
20 Mortimer Street,
London W1T 3JW

First published by Welbeck in 2021

A CIP catalogue record for this book is available from the British Library

ISBN
Trade Paperback 978-1787399594

Typeset by Roger Walker

Printed in Great Britain by CPI Books, Chatham, Kent

10 9 8 7 6 5 4 3 2 1

The Forest Stewardship Council® is an international nongovernmental
organization that promotes environmentally appropriate, socially beneficial,
and economically viable management of the world's forests.
To learn more, visit www.fsc.org

www.welbeckpublishing.com

DEDICATION

For my Ed, Max, Maddy and Marina

Acknowledgements

Thanking as always my family, Ed, Max, Maddy and Marina who know to stay clear of me when I'm in a writing frenzy and still love me when it's over.

Ajda Vucicevic from Welbeck who published the book and saw the urgency to print it quickly for those affected by the recent emotionally turbulent roller coaster ride and want to find the brakes.

Caroline Michel – my agent who pushed this baby to fruition.

And the brilliant Bella Pollen who edited this book. Without her you wouldn't have understood a word – she took chaos and moulded it into sense.

Special credit to Gareth Dauncey who is in the process of creating an app called Mood and who created this exercise idea in the book.

EXERCISE:
Keeping track of change.
On the page you'll see a calendar with all the days of the month on it.

Choose 10 colours from your crayons and put them in the order of the mood they evoke. Decide which are the feel-good, positive colours and which are the feeling crap, negative colours, i.e. you decide yellow for positive is 1, green for less great is 4, maybe beige is neither positive or negative at 5. And then the colours get darker until black = 10.

Each day when you wake up, choose which colour your mood is and scribble it onto the day on the calendar. You can also do it before you go to sleep at night.

At the end of a week or month, notice how your colours changed day by day. If they've stayed black for over a week, you've probably got depression.

Contents

Introduction

If anyone had told us a few weeks before March 2020 that most of the world would be unable to leave their homes because a virus was going on a rampage, we would have said it was a bad idea for a script. But suddenly, as it dawned on us this might be more than a rumour, we realised we were going to a showdown at high noon with our deepest fears. There were no information packs for what to do in this kind of emergency, so we headed for our homes and hunkered down – alone and traumatised.

One of the reasons we were so ill-prepared for this recent existential slap in the face is that we were suddenly forced to confront the harsh truths of difficult emotions, uncertainty, loneliness, change, dissatisfaction and death. In other words, the cold hard facts of life.

I don't want to get into "should haves" (we already think those words too often and they don't do us any good). But it would have saved us a lot of despair if we'd been more aware of these "realities", not only for the pandemic, but generally, and especially when the time comes to face our termination.

These six realities – I will call them the Big Six throughout this book – should have been tattooed on some visible part of our bodies so they could never have taken us by surprise. We should have been taught to deal with them during our first years in school (in a child-friendly way). From now on, parents should be fined for negligence if they fail to teach us about them. Maybe they could gently but honestly tell us that the fish died and what that means, rather than just telling us our fish went on a holiday.

It's not as if you won't have heard of the Big Six. It's that, like most of us, you probably choose not to think about them too much. I mean, why upset yourself and ruin a perfectly nice day? Maybe we humans don't want to face them head on, because if we did, our lives might just grind to a halt. What would be worth doing if nothing was permanent? Why throw everything we've got into anything if nothing is certain? If every second is a possible end, why begin anything? Of course, deep down, we know everything changes, everything is uncertain, we're alone, we die – blah! blah! blah! But who wants to go there when there's so much on Netflix to watch? This isn't a culture that likes to emotionally dig down, so we make sure we lock the existential closet and bury the keys.

Then there may be some people thinking, "I'm fully booked. I can't possibly think about stuff like dying. I just haven't got the time." We try to avoid anything unpleasant or painful, not realising that when the realities finally do land on our doorstep (and they will), they will take us down and render us completely useless.

For a long time now, we've been too busy to notice disturbing realities because we were all on tight schedules of "must do" things, most of which were things that didn't ever need to be done. So many of our deadlines are self-imposed to keep the adrenaline pumping, to give us a sense of purpose and importance. We'll do anything rather than look too deeply into ourselves, so any diversion is appreciated.

Before the pandemic, we didn't notice much of anything. Glued to our digital rectangles; our heads permanently sucked into cyberspace. I think the culprit was Microsoft Office when, 10 years ago, it said, "You can now take your workplace anywhere," and that was the end of having time to be screenless, having time for ourselves; having time to find out what might make us happy, how we liked living our life or just give it some meaning. The curse of Microsoft Office came true. The office is now in our bed, bath, on our holiday, while walking, jogging, eating, on planes, trains and automobiles. It's with us while we watch babies being born and even at funerals while someone's being buried.

For all our time-saving devices, we've still had to speed up our lives to keep up with so much incoming. Why can't we let computers do what they were meant to do and leave us alone to have a nice time: learning shuffleboard or designing yurts or whatever would make us happy? Why shouldn't *they*, not us, have to hit deadlines? Surely some coder could code the computer to burn out rather than us?

Now we're at the beck and call of our machines. Waiting for them to ping so we can immediately ping back. It's like a horrible game of tennis that never ends – where you die of exhaustion with love points. We can't really blame anyone. We're party to our own downfall. We complain we have no time to ourselves but then choose to live surrounded by weapons of mass distraction.

If we ever switch off, we say, "We're killing time." Then we get frightened because no one is pinging us, and that's when the hunt for distraction really kicks in hard. The truth is we're afraid of having time because we have no idea what to do with it. Even while we complain about not having enough, we make every moment a record-breaking dash to the next and then wonder where it all went.

In the same way, we complain about always being online, yet we're addicted to online because normal time feels too slow – and God forbid we might get bored. Nothing tastes as good as that rush of adrenaline when you can order something that can be delivered faster than the speed of light. Even watching the cartoon of a tiny Uber coming to pick me up gets me high.

Without being aware, we've sold our souls and data to the devil as a two-for-one. Google knows more about me than I ever will.

But what would happen if we stopped and became more aware of what it is to be alive? Maybe take our focus from always seeking something *outside* to seeking something *inside* ourselves? Get to know who we are, which we definitely won't find in our inbox. I'm not suggesting we dump tech. Are you crazy? I'm on it right now, obviously. Or how would I be writing this book? A typewriter? A plume? Get out of here.

We're **addicted** to **online** because **normal time** feels too **slow**

All I'm saying is that we need to find a counterbalance to our turbulent inner world. To slow it down so we have time to check in with ourselves (and not through voicemail), to examine what really matters.

The fact is, many of us were asleep at the wheel when it came to the pandemic. In March 2020, all Big Six realities were smashed into our faces in one fell swoop. Out of the blue, we were locked into our own homes with nothing to face but an uncertain future with, horror of horrors, no distractions. We were all mutually forced to go cold turkey off our busyness, which meant we had to be alone with our own thoughts. Oh my God, we suddenly saw ourselves naked, with no masks to hide behind, no personalities to jack up, no parties to be invited to, with never having to dress up (especially our lower halves) to look good.

I found myself with a front row seat on all this. Every evening, I watched people sitting at home being helplessly torpedoed by one reality check after another. Throughout the day and probably most of the night too, they were on an emotional roller coaster, forced to face difficult emotions, uncertainty, loneliness, change, dissatisfaction and death all at once.

I witnessed this daily onslaught because I was running something called the Frazzled Cafe.

Frazzled Cafes

Four years ago, I wanted to create something like AA for anyone with a form of burnout. A place where you could meet in a safe environment with a small group of people who would still love you when you took off the mask and unbolted the armour. I wanted to create a place where people could get real, cut the bullshit and not have to bark back the word "fine" when asked how they were. Previously, I crashed a few AA meetings, which I loved, because everyone was on the same alcoholic page. Unfortunately, the meeting I was at didn't encourage my return when I fessed up that I wasn't an addict. They were nice but really I was sort of the wrong species for them. Since when do you have to audition to prove that you're fucked up?

But I got their point, so I thought I'd start my own group for those of us who feel "frazzled" and wanted to meet others of the same ilk. This wasn't to be a group for people who all suffered with mental illness – that would have to be run by professional therapists. But I wanted to create a community where we could just talk without the usual agenda to impress, provoke or prove something; speak straight from the heart without fear that we might be boring to someone or seemingly weak.

Frazzled Cafes began life in Marks & Spencer. They supported us and opened their cafes for meetings up and down the UK. We invited small groups of about 12 to 15 people (the perfect number for a nomadic family). They would meet regularly every two weeks with a facilitator who was there to listen, make everyone feel safe, and begin and end the meetings with a few minutes of mindfulness to help de-frazzle the room.

By the way, I didn't make up the word. To be in a state of "frazzle" is a neurological function meaning, "A constant stress overloading the nervous system, flooding it with cortisol and adrenaline. The attention of the frazzled person is fixed on what's worrying them and not the job in hand, which can lead to burnout."

Being frazzled is a contemporary ailment where we're not just stressed, anxious and fearful, but we have a simultaneous internal commentary running inside our heads badgering us with, "I shouldn't be stressed. No one else is this anxious. I'm such a loser to be this scared."

So, the commonality of the M&S cafes was that we were all in the same state and wanted to help each other and ourselves.

There, we provided hot and cold running trust and rapport, allowing everyone to do what humans do best – bond.

And it worked.

The cafe met every two weeks, and some people stayed with their group for four years and are all still in touch.

They said that their small groups were a lifeline to sanity, because in this bizarre world of ours, people don't want to tell their friends and family what's really going on. They don't want to be a burden. Our ancestors sitting around the fire would have thought this hysterical, and even more hysterical to them would be the idea of humans needing shrinks.

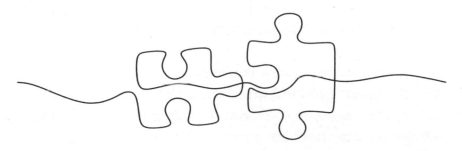

Frazzled Cafes during lockdown

When the pandemic started, the Frazzled Cafe went online and I began to lead nightly Zoom meetings for groups of about 80 people.

During lockdown, we were being blitzed by the Big Six realities day and night. New people joined and began speaking about their fears, maybe for the first time in their lives. What was so terrifying with the pandemic was that in war you know where the bombs are falling, but this was an invisible enemy and even friends were potential virus snipers. When I was out and saw kids walking at me, I'd think "incoming" and go hide in a hedge.

So, all of us had the wake-up call of wake-up calls – that our lives weren't a rehearsal we were casually strolling through, with a lot of tea breaks. Our lives were actually the real performance and now we had to make decisions fast. Decisions we'd never had to make before, like: If we could only see three people who would they be? Who did we want to go into lockdown with? Who did we want to get out of lockdown with? Who did we really care about and want to call? Who did we never want to hear from again?

We even had to think about whether we had married the right person, whether we wanted to change our lives, make peace with anyone before it was too late. Many of us realised if we did nothing and just sat it out, we'd be living like snails smearing ourselves up and down the fish tank, pointing in any which way, going nowhere slowly.

While people were thinking about those hard-core, smack-in-your-face topics, I was learning about the human race fast and how we react in the crossfire. Running those nightly meetings, I had the privilege of being a confidante and friend to a cross section of the population. It felt like I was taking the pulse of the nation as we were challenged by the full catastrophe of those realities.

During the day, we also had hosts running smaller meetings. Who knew that technology would come up trumps? After all our complaining, now it was our greatest source for intimacy. On screen, you couldn't be distracted by tech because you were using tech. So when someone spoke, all eyes were on them, fully engaged and fully present. We had people of all ages, ethnicities, gender, nationalities – when someone spoke, you saw these heads from all over the world, nodding as if to say, "Yes, I feel that way too."

In my opinion, emotions are just as visceral and contagious online as in person. Love, hate, sex, envy, fear, and more, are just as transmittable on a screen. Otherwise, why would we watch films? And at all meetings, the compassion was infectious – everyone caught it.

After doing a few minutes of mindfulness, I always began asking people to give us the weather conditions in their minds. They knew exactly what I meant, and people spoke for only a minute or two, uncensored and honestly. You could hear a communal sigh of relief each time someone spoke, recognising that we all felt the same way.

Almost every night, tired and confused, I thought, "Why am I running this? I have so many things I should be doing." And each night when I finished those meetings, I knew why. I felt so strongly that I was with my people. Strangely, I felt closer to the attendees at Frazzled than some people I've known for 20 or more years.

At almost every session, the attendees thanked me for creating Frazzled and giving them a place to be heard, but I always said the same thing: that whatever they were getting out of it, I was getting even more. For me, no theatre, concert or book can ever give me that feeling I get from Frazzled – that sense of communal embrace, like our hearts are all chained together on the human charm bracelet. These people might be strangers when the meeting starts, but by the time it's ended, I love them because they're brave enough to show me a little piece of who they are.

So for a while now, I've been a proxy to this human roller coaster, riding with all my people in the same car – arms up and screaming with them as we plummet into hell, teeth bared before we slowly climb back up. I've had a bird's-eye view of how humans deal with the Big Six. What makes them survive? And what makes them sink under? And all this has been the inspiration behind *A Mindfulness Guide for Survival*.

About this workbook

As I begin writing this workbook, it's still lockdown. It's anyone's guess whether by the time it's published, the pandemic will be over (this one anyway) and we'll all be skipping in the streets, kissing each other like at the end of WW2 – or maybe we'll all still be hunkered at home, shaking in our boots from the trauma of it all.

Wherever we are, I'm writing this in case we're ever caught with our emotional pants down again. I'm writing it for me *and* for you, to try to steady and strengthen our mind muscles to be able to take on the slings and arrows of whatever outrageous fortune comes at us in the future.

I offer it as a guide to help bulk up our emotional resilience as far as learning to deal with the unknown. So that when the waves of living feel unswimmable, and we feel we're going under, there are enough life jackets to go round.

This isn't just a "how to survive post-pandemic", this is for survival in general – how to get through a day without thinking we've failed, that we didn't do enough, that we should have or could have ... (well, you know the lyrics). I'm writing this to remind you that who we are *is* enough. And that if we can believe that, if we can create a calmer environment *inside* us, this will impact on what's *outside* us, too.

When we complain about how crowded, polluted and disorganised our world is, we need to remember it didn't start off that way. Duh! The world we're looking at now is the manifestation of how we feel inside – and it won't change until we change ourselves. The world doesn't need healing – *we* do.

I'm writing this book because I know that when we feel connected to our bodies and minds, it's as if we've found home. And when we find home, things like uncertainty and loneliness don't pack the same punch. The outside world may be in chaos, but if we know we've always got the house of "us" to come back to, we will always have a refuge.

The aim of this book is to help you find that refuge, or at least help you build one. To do that, we have to be fearless, bring dark realities out into the light and accept them. This takes courage and effort, and most people would rather just "have a nice day". But we've seen what happens when the days stop being so nice. We know we need some kind of safety net so the fall doesn't kill us. None of us want to face the unfaceable, but there has to be a baptism of fire if we're to come out the other end – wise, not broken.

So let's take our first hard look at the inevitable together. That's what I'm here for.

When we feel **connected** to our bodies and minds, it's as if we've found **home**

The "Big Six" realities

Reality one: Difficult emotions

These have always been part of our repertoire, but they became the norm during lockdown, relentlessly firing at us: sadness, anxiety, panic, fear, shame, guilt, loss … "To feel" is what makes us human.

If we try to suppress emotions:
A) they won't work
B) sooner or later, they will ultimately express themselves and it won't be pretty.

Emotions tend to explode out of us when we least expect them.

Reality two: Uncertainty

There are few guarantees in this world. We're certain that gravity works and most of us are carbon-based. Outside that, I wouldn't place any bets.

No one wants to feel like the world is a rug that's about to be pulled out from under them. This state wasn't a new thing; we experienced all those attributes before the virus hit. We were blissfully unaware that nothing was certain – which, of course, is the only truth there is.

Reality three: Loneliness

During the pandemic, so many people said they felt alone as if experiencing loneliness for the first time. We were always alone but we kept ourselves busy, so we never needed to face the music. Connected by our fingertips to the world gave us the illusion that we were all part of a community with so much in common. We weren't – and we aren't.

It's not enough to feel connected to others because you both like the same settee or everyone gives a thumbs up to a photo of someone's lunch. Maybe all this imposed loneliness has given us a wake-up call to do what humans do best: mingle and bond. Hopefully, from now on, we can start to care about each other rather than care about what each of us does for a living, how old we look, how firm we feel or what designer label we're wearing.

Even among **friends**, family and loved ones, you are **alone**

Reality four: Change

Seasons change, the world turns, time moves forward and we get older (not me but all of you). Even if you rage against the night, before you finish reading this sentence billions of your cells have died and new ones are reborn.

Why, oh why can't we remain young or stay in love forever? We can't. Impermanence is the law of the universe. Hold onto your pants because time moves and we are never the same from one second to the next.

Reality five: Dissatisfaction

Humans can't get it into their heads that they should want what they have, instead of have what they want. It's this endless craving that brings us to our knees with frustration and blows our self-esteem to smithereens.

We're on a drip feed of envy, with images shoved in our faces of glistening people, living the life we never will. They're probably miserable too, but we rarely get that news. Social media makes us yearn to be someone else, and it makes that someone else also yearn to be someone else ... the yearning never stops.

Reality six: Death

Death is the mother of all reality checks. Though you may be the buffest on the block, with the neural firing of a Tesla and everyone loves you – even your kids – the one thing you can depend on is that it all eventually goes. I'm not here to bum you out, but like the Girl Scouts taught me – "Be prepared". You can only savour moments of your life if you hold the thought and remember that we all have a sell-by date – just like yogurt.

The Big Six realities

Write down, in order, which of the Big Six realities upset you most – and why.

(We might all put death as number one, but you never know. You may be a Buddhist – to them, it's just a change of clothes.)

1 ....
....

2 ....
....

3 ....
....

4 ....
....

5 ....
....

6 ....
....

Why we feel helpless in the face of the Big Six

We used to have communities to fall back on. We used to have big family units that stuck together through thick and thin. We had elders who passed down their wisdom to us. We had religion to explain the bad stuff away, and a god to hide behind. Now, many of us don't know our neighbours, and town halls are closed or used for antique sales, meaning buying the same crap back that we threw out. Our relatives are scattered to the wind. And as for our wise elders? How do you recognise them once they've had Botox?

Then there's God...

Right from the start humans knew they needed something bigger than themselves to deal with the unknown. The Greeks and Romans didn't have to face any realities. All uncertainties could be explained by the gods' and goddesses' behaviours. If there was a disaster, people weren't frightened – they just assumed Zeus was having a hissy fit, throwing his thunderbolts around.

The Jews believed God would always protect them, feeling safe that he had their backs. When Pharaoh refused to allow them to exit Egypt, God took over and sent in not one, but ten plagues: floods, rivers of blood, frogs by the millions ... Each time Pharaoh refused to play ball, God kept 'em coming ... pestilence, boils, raining locusts and, finally, the crème de la crème – death to all the first born. And so off they skipped to the Promised Land.

Enter Jesus. He said he'd wash away all our sins if we followed his word – if not, we'd go straight to hell. Pretty clear messaging, I'd say. That's probably why he was so popular. Once again, we didn't have to lift a finger. We just had to believe.

When religion was bad – i.e. being hung, drawn, quartered, burnt, dismembered or spiked to name but a few – it caused way more pain and suffering than relief.

But when religion was good, it was very, very good, giving people meaning, community, safety, certainty and compassion.

Buddhism isn't an organised religion – it's a way of training the mind, enabling you to find the answers for yourself

So here we are in the 21st century with religion losing its popularity. We feel rudderless and exposed to the unknown. It seems like no one is out there helping us find a little peace and happiness.

Around 2,500 years ago, some guy called Siddhartha was suddenly hit by exactly the same Big Six realities I'm talking about in this workbook. See ... we aren't the first people to get hit with those. He searched inside himself and found the answer, which was to free the mind, and that's how Buddhism began.

Buddhism isn't an organised religion. Religion, as I've stated, hasn't worked out for everyone. But it's a way of training the mind (mindfulness), and enables you to find the answers for yourself without God making all the decisions.

My qualifications

I know nothing about warding off another virus, crisis intervention or negotiating with a member of the Taliban, but I do know what to do with the mind. Not because I'm a naturally born "Enlightened One", but because I studied, practised and still practise mindfulness. I've been judiciously exercising my brain, giving me the tools to surf the emotional tsunamis (and they come at me on the hour).

It's thanks to mindfulness that I can sense when a depression is about to rear its demonic head, suck out my soul and leave me like an empty glove puppet. Mindfulness gives me the clarity to prepare myself and take precautions. I've learned to be kind to myself by treating my depression as a serious mental illness that needs kindness and care, not some self-indulgent cry for attention as those remaining stigmatisers still believe.

Why I went for mindfulness

I'm a sceptic, so anything too dream-catchery or "ting ting" wind-chimey, means I'm outta there fast. It was the science that originally attracted me to mindfulness. The fact that it was possible to visibly map how a living brain functions was a showstopper for me.

I was hooked, so I headed to Oxford – as you do when you're in your fifties – to get myself a Master's degree in mindfulness-based cognitive therapy. At Oxford, I could peek into MRI scanners and observe how a brain could change after practising mindfulness for even a few weeks.

Richard Davidson, the first neuroscientist to, with the permission of the Dalai Lama, scan the brains of long practising monks, said in his early research, "An increasing number of brain-imaging MRI studies of the impact of mindfulness suggest that it reliably and profoundly alters the structure and function of the brain to improve the quality of both thoughts and feelings. It appears to reshape the neural pathways, increasing density and complexity of connections in areas associated with cognitive abilities such as attention, self-awareness, introspection and areas connected with kindness and compassion. All this while decreasing density in the amygdala (the alarm button of the brain) therefore decreasing panic, anxiety, fear and fury."

By the time I was in my fifties, I was a permanent resident in those negative emotions. I thought it was impossible for me to even contemplate living in the world with peace or ease – not with my background.

I come from generations of immigrants who always felt chased, and were literally being chased, who survived by living on a high-octane diet of panic and rage. Why would I stand a chance to break this inherited Wax cycle of "get out of the Ghetto and get out fast" mentality? We Waxes were always quick packers. We could move a piano across Lithuania in minutes if we had to run.

A Mindfulness Guide for Survival – A Workbook

Once you buy this book, it's up to you what you do with it.
Please feel free to rip it up, re-gift it, use it as wallpaper. But to
get the best out of it, if I were you, I'd pick it up once every day,
or whenever you're feeling frazzled, follow the exercises and
fill in the questionnaires. (You will also need a pen, pencil and
crayons.) I promise you'll get to know yourself and, even better,
you'll get to like yourself too.

This workbook isn't just about how to get through a pandemic
and its post-pandemic fallout. It's also a wake-up call, to
become aware of every moment you have the privilege of
existing on this earth.

So scribble in it, doodle in it – take it with you everywhere.
No one but you is going to see what's inside it. This isn't only
a self-help book or a colouring book. Think of it as an "evolve
yourself" book.

If you use this book, I promise you that next time there's a
catastrophe – from a small-scale one (your dog is missing, or
you forgot to return an email) to another big world crisis (the

spread of a future variant caused by people in Utah eating aliens) – you'll be ready.

Even if nothing apocalyptic ever happens again in your lifetime, use this book as a guide on how to drop anchor when your life – and the world – gets too daunting. The way I figure it is, we're all in the same storm, just in different boats. And I hope this book can help you hold the rudder straight, no matter how turbulent the waves, and come out the other end buoyant.

This isn't **only** a
self-help book or a
colouring book.
Think of it as an
"evolve yourself"
book

Mindfulness – why should you do it?

Mindfulness is about learning what's going on in your mind, in the present, with compassion and without beating yourself up. If you practise the exercises in this book while having fun doodling and colouring, it might just become your tool of tools for holding onto your mind, while all around you people are losing theirs. It may look from the outside that you're doing nothing more than sitting on some gluten-free cushion with your eyes shut tight, but inside you're exercising regions in your brain that strengthen your ability to focus your attention, reduce stress, gain insight, experience presence and increase compassion.

If you haven't practised or studied mindfulness before, now is the perfect time, while so many of us are rethinking how we want to live in the future. We need to do something if we want to change how we think, feel and act – it won't happen through wishful thinking.

Why should anything happen automatically? Everything we've ever learned is by rote, from walking to talking to learning any sport or any skill. It takes training and repetition, but we can train our brains to stop giving us such a hard time and show us some joy. With a conscious decision, we can recalibrate our minds, making them the greatest place to live in on earth; our gold-medal Condé Nast Traveller destination of choice. That's my definition of happiness.

Sorting out your closet

My aim is to help sort out your mind in the same way you'd sort out your closet – like the feng shui of the mental health world. I'll help you figure out what no longer fits and what to replace it with. It's hard to stand back, get a clear view of your own mind and figure out how to organise it. It's nearly impossible to be conscious of what you're not conscious of. Or, as Albert Einstein said, "No problem can be solved from the same level of consciousness that created it." Al and I think the same.

Recalibrating your mind

Many people say, "Why should I tidy my closet? I don't care if it's a mess, it is what it is and I haven't got the time/strength/interest to do anything about it." The state of our closet doesn't really affect us – we can live with it. But the state of our mind

Mindfulness training makes it **possible** for you to observe the **contents** of your **mind**

determines if we're having a nice life or a life in hell, and if we're happy or not.

I'm pretty sure it might be worth putting in some effort to do whatever we need to do to clear up our minds. The question is, can it be done?

I've said it before, and I'll say it a million more times – "The brain is a moveable feast." You can break unhelpful, negative mental habits and create more positive, uplifting ones; it's all in your mind (not your hands, as the saying suggests).

You can no longer get away with saying, "I am what I am." Those lyrics have to be dumped and replaced with, "The brain is made up of about 82 billion neurons making trillions of connections, continuously changing partners based on our moment-to-moment thoughts and experiences. This is known as neuroplasticity." It's probably not going to be a hit song, but it's all true.

"The **brain** is a **moveable** feast." You can break unhelpful, **negative** mental habits and create more **positive**, **uplifting** ones

You also can't say any more, "I'm stuck with these genes." Even that excuse has been taken away from us by scientific evidence. I grew up thinking we came into the world pre-packaged, at the mercy of our genetic blueprint. It turns out the genes just give you the raw scaffolding. How you ultimately build on that scaffolding is up to you.

You're the architect of your own life, so you can't blame the world for how you ended up. So even your genes can change depending on how you experience the world and therefore how you think. Google "epigenetics".

I love a challenge, and the idea of re-calibrating my brain was the biggest gauntlet ever thrown down to me – by me. I found it incredible that without the magic of medication or surgery, I could actually re-landscape my own forest of neurons and give my genes a makeover. What a versatile miracle we humans are. At Oxford, I learned that all this rebuilding of neurons and reshuffling of genes can be done through the practice of mindfulness, so I jumped on that bandwagon and have been clutching on tight ever since.

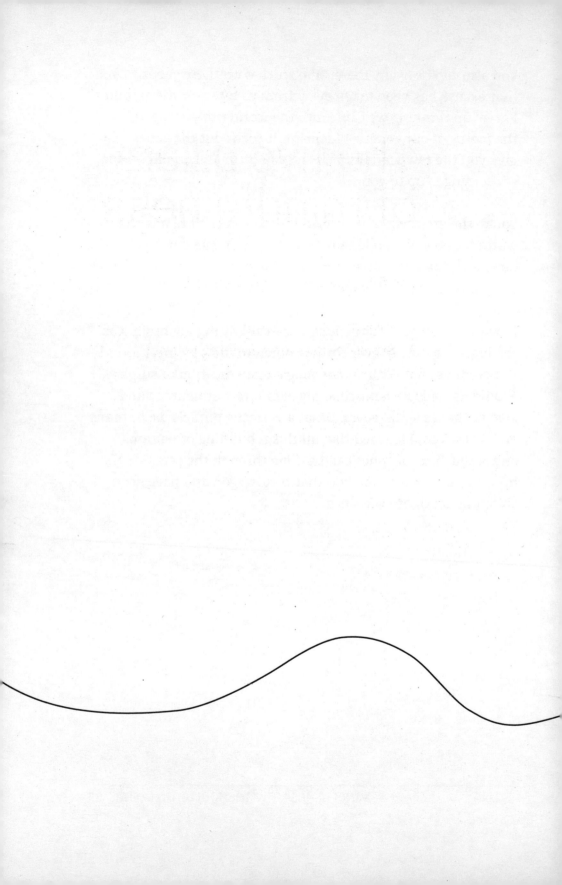

The five pillars of mindfulness

The five pillars of mindfulness are:

1   **Insight**
2   **Stress reduction/grounding yourself**
3   **Emotional awareness**
4   **Presence**
5   **Kindness**

Pillar one: Insight

Getting to know you

The first step of mindfulness is about introducing you to how your mind works. Most of us assume our mind knows what it's doing. But it actually has no clue. It usually takes us up blind alleys where we hit a wall trying to figure out why life is unfair, why we can't have what we want and who or what's getting in the way of our happiness.

This egocentric point of view means we believe we are the centre of the universe and should be treated accordingly. So we defend our views and feel justified declaring war on anyone who thinks otherwise. This is why the world is in trouble. Because we forget that no one else see things the way we do – but really, why should they?

Our bespoke reality

We believe that our thoughts and emotions are reasonable responses to some solid outside reality. Lesson number one is that there's no unified, single reality out there.

Each of us has a completely different lens through which we see the world and ourselves. Everything we think and feel is based on our personal cocktail of memories, our parents or caregivers, our experiences, genes and habits. No two people on earth have the same reality. Think of a car accident; every witness has their interpretation of the events. Even a judge with the bang of a hammer can only make a semi-informed guess at the truth.

Getting to know thyself

From way back in Greece, some of you may remember Socrates mentioning, "An unexamined life is not worth living." But did we listen? No, we didn't. And this is why now, after so many years, we're floundering around trying to figure out not who we are, but who we want to be like.

We know our subjective beliefs and stick to them, like the common one – "I'm not good enough" – but that's about as far as we get. Who we really are below the labels remains a mystery.

People in the past looked for meaning in their lives, but somewhere along the way it went out of fashion. Philosophers were unemployable so no one went down that career route. Existentialists were onto something, but in the end they just hung out in cafes and smoked themselves to death. It's time we brought all this deep thinking back from the past – this getting to know yourself thing – because in my book that's the only road to happiness.

You probably won't know who you are at the end of these exercises, but they may give you a taster of how much more there is, besides the few labels you've used to define yourself.

"Getting to know yourself" exercise

Exercise 1: Who are you?

Answer these questions, but each time you ask yourself the question, write something different so you don't repeat your answers.

1   Who am I?

....

2   Write something you didn't use to answer question one.

....

3   Ask yourself again: Who am I?

....

4   Write something else you didn't use to answer question two.

....

5   Ask yourself again: Who am I?

....

Firstly, all of the answers you've given are correct. I know we humans always think we're being tested so, yes, you've passed.

The point is to show you that we're not our job, our schooling, our clothes, our status, our personality, how smart we are, how pretty we are, our colour, our age, our shoe size ... We are far more than the descriptions we give ourselves. Our thoughts and feelings ebb and flow. We are works in progress, always shape-shifting like a pile of sand in the desert being blown in the wind.

Who we think we are is based on habits of thinking that we've picked up along the way. These habits aren't who we are, but because we've repeated them so often we convince ourselves they are. And as far as neuroplasticity goes, the more you repeat a thought, the more hard-wired those neuronal connections get – and it becomes more and more difficult to break free.

Exercise 2: What are your thinking habits?

Which internal phrases are most familiar to you? (These are my top ones – add your own.)

★ I'm not good enough.
★ No one cares about me.
★ I'm so selfish.
★ I'm too needy.
★ I should have, could have...
★ ....
★ ....
★ ....
★ ....
★ ....
★ ....
★ ....

Which of these styles describe your thinking when under stress?

☐ Catastrophising – everything that happens to me is the worst that can happen.

☐ Self blame – everything that happens is my fault.

☐ Finding someone else to blame.

☐ Going numb – your body and brain shut down.

☐ Brain-bombing – relentless incoming of "Should do, could do, didn't do..."

The only way we can discern how narrow our views are, and how biased we are, is by becoming aware of what our mind is bringing to the table. If we're not conscious of this, we won't realise how trapped we are in these judgments, like a record caught in a groove, endlessly replaying itself.

Exercise 3: How to check if you're stuck in a groove

A friend of yours passes you on the street and doesn't notice you. What would be your reaction? Some people might think the friend was preoccupied or just had eye surgery and didn't see them. My default mode is thinking she's ignoring me, she's figured out who I really am and doesn't like what she sees.

Write down how you would respond if a friend passed you on the street and didn't notice you. What would you be thinking?

★ She hates me (mine).

★ She's just had eye surgery and didn't see me.

★ She's thinking about something else and didn't see me.

★ She's trying to ignore me because I've upset her (another one of mine).

★ She doesn't notice anyone.

Where our habits come from

When we were young, our parents or teachers often put us in a box labelled "smart", "stupid", "slow", "lazy" etc. and hammered the lid shut. (The last three were repeatedly scrawled over my early report cards.) We tend to accept these labels and run with them for the rest of our lives.

We can also get stuck in habits because friends don't like to see that we have changed. None of us want to disappoint so we pretend to be who we used to be and get stuck in the past. This is why some people you went to school with might still be calling you "Piggy" when you're 56.

Some of our habits are highly addictive so they're difficult to let go of. When we allow that anger to soar through our veins, it gives us an adrenaline high. But afterwards, guess who gets ill? Not the receiver of our fury. We do. We're the ones with the hangover – poisoned by our own toxins. This is called "drinking the poison and hoping our enemy will die".

Samples of my labels are:

★ sad sack (thanks Dad)
★ not pretty (thanks Mum)
★ stupid (all teachers gave me that one)
★ a loser (kids in the playground)
★ bossy (kids at my camp)

Exercise 4: What are your labels?

Write down your labels and who gave them to you (if you remember).

1 ....

2 ....

3 ....

4 ....

5 ....

6 ....

7 ....

8 ....

So how do you break your mental and emotional habits?

Once you're aware of your more critical themes, and how often you use them, you might start to notice that your judgment is skewed. How can we stand outside ourselves and be able to discern which thoughts are true and which are just old recordings?

All is not lost – we have an innate ability to observe our thoughts, emotions and bodily sensations. You're the first to feel when you've eaten too much, you're heartbroken or you've stubbed your toe.

All of us can insert a periscope inside ourselves and take a visceral selfie of what's going on below the surface. The problem comes when we beat ourselves up for those very feelings and thoughts. The critical thinker enters and gives us the worst reviews known to man. This is where mindfulness steps in. The training is all about helping us see the contents of our minds objectively, without judging ourselves and with self-compassion because, without those, we'll just find more things to be critical about.

One way to not break a habit is by shouting, "You idiot, you've done it again!" at yourself when you recognise you've made a mistake. This will only embed your habit deeper.

If you get angry at yourself, that stress starts bubbling. And the more it bubbles, the harder and quicker your mind digs in its heels and goes back to the old default mode. We give ourselves grief for getting angry so it starts to pick up speed with, "Why do I always fail?" "I'm not good enough" "It's my mother's fault."

You'll keep trying to figure out the answers, except there aren't any. You won't sleep, you won't be able to concentrate, you'll lose your temper, and your friends and family will probably lose theirs, too. You may even make yourself physically ill because you're now in the world of the frazzled. The very thing that could have saved you, i.e. your rational mind, is out of commission.

It isn't easy when it comes to looking into ourselves and confronting our demons, but unless we become mindful of them, they remain a permanent fixture. The more we're unaware how much they influence every decision and action, the more stuck we become. We look around and innocently say, "I didn't do anything," not realising we did everything, especially the damage.

We are the creators of this rock-solid self-imposed identity and assume that what we experience is reality, that what we believe is fact, and should someone dare to disagree, we become self-righteous and confrontational. There's no outside reality, only our own manufactured one – and the more practised our habits become, the more we're slaves to them.

Let's say my reaction is repeatedly angry for most situations. Eventually, I become proficient at anger and I'll make every excuse in the world why I'm justified to feel it. I know this one, because for most of my life I was addicted to anger and would make a habit of hunting down victims who I believed were either stupid or trying to screw me over. I would intentionally scare them with my aggression to such an extent that they made mistakes, at which point I had a legitimate excuse to pummel them even more. I was like an angry cat torturing a mouse.

As with anything, practice makes perfect. I'm sure if you get angry for about 10,000 hours, you'll become an expert. Each time you repeat a thought or feeling, you're reinforcing those synaptic networks in your brain, which become more and more difficult to untangle, until you've locked yourself in a home-made prison built for one.

If something goes wrong in our lives, very few of us are prepared to look inside ourselves to locate our contribution.

If you want to understand evil, love, terror, war, revenge, bigotry and savagery, inside is where you have to look. We're all carriers, however hard we try and point the finger at everyone else. These things aren't somewhere out there or caused by the Big Bang, they come from us. If we become aware of these dark materials, we'll be able to choose how to express them, rather than unconsciously project them onto some innocent person.

Only when we're at peace with ourselves, can we possibly transform bigotry into compassion. If we act without awareness, we may be planting the seeds for another disaster. This is why the terrorised become the terrorists, believing their anger and revenge is justified. We all know these things deep down but it's so much easier and more exciting to find a common enemy and join in that almost euphoric collective anger.

Building awareness

We all have an innate ability to observe our thoughts, emotions and bodily sensations. Mindfulness gives us self-awareness, which is the only thing that can unlock bad habits.

When we're aware of something, we're not at the mercy of it. To be in the grip of sweat-dripping, hair-raising fear is a vastly different condition than being aware of that fear. It's like our mind steps back and says "I'm watching you" to the fear, which weakens it. When you know you're scared, you're not so scared. And the same with all the other emotions.

Sometimes, you're naturally aware – say, when there's an emergency, like your house is on fire, or someone you love gets ill or something out of the ordinary, whether beautiful or shocking, grabs your attention. These are easy to recognise. They're visuals. They exist outside of us, but with an emotion signalling us from inside, we're usually too preoccupied to notice.

We need to train ourselves to place our attention where we want it, when we want it, not wait for it to grab us. If you're

Mindfulness gives us
self-awareness,
which is the only thing
that can unlock **bad habits**

---

thinking, "What's she going on about, I know how to pay attention," here's an example of how little control we have over our own attention. Just in case you think you've got a handle on yours.

Focusing our attention

- ★ **Focus** on something that catches your eye close to where you're sitting. Notice how long it takes before your mind pulls you away.
- ★ **Focus** on the sound around you. Notice how long it takes before your mind pulls you away.
- ★ **Now focus** your mind on something you love – your pet, kids, friend, partner ... See how long you can stay with it before your mind pulls you away.

See what I mean? Our ability to focus attention isn't our finest asset. Our thoughts make all the decisions, and this can easily usurp our desires. If you lose focus on sight and sound, you can survive, sure, but isn't it something of a tragedy when you can't focus on what you love?

So, I think I've made it clear that we're out of shape when it comes to being aware. We all have the mental equipment under our hoods to be able to focus, but if it were that easy we wouldn't be in this state.

Mindfulness offers a way out. The first thing it helps us do is lower the fear. We can't begin to focus when we're drowning in that red mist of vigilance waiting for the next threat. We can't think straight so we cling onto our bad habits for dear life, because better the devil we know. To change, to mess with our identity, is too daunting. So we remain victims of our mad, bad thoughts, constantly allowing them to machine gun us down, never mind how painful or destructive it is.

We need to dump the fear, lower our cortisol ("stress hormone") levels, otherwise we'll never break free from that nagging mother of a mind. (In my case, it really *is* the voice of my mother nagging me.) With practice, you learn to sit back and observe your mind with coolness and calm as that parade of thoughts (or the shitshow, as I like to call it) goes by.

Neuroscience and mindfulness

I love the sciency bit of mindfulness, because nothing is as joyous as when I'm looking into a scanner and watching how a brain can change with training. Watching any brain is always sexy to me, but watching how it can alter with mindfulness training is my heart-throb. This is done by placing someone who's a practitioner of mindfulness in an fMRI scanner and asking them to do specific tasks or think specific thoughts and then noting if neurons in various areas are activated or not.

I had my brain scanned in an fMRI at the end of writing *A Mindfulness Guide for the Frazzled* and reported the results in the book's last chapter. I was scanned before and after a week's silent mindfulness retreat. The results were impressive. It was reassuring to know that with all that practice I've put in (not just that week but years), my brain had some of the traits of a well-trained brain. If nothing else is buff on me, at least I know my brain is.

What happens in your brain?

When thoughts are rampaging in your head, it means a region in your brain called the amygdala is activated. That's your amygdala's job – to alert you to possible danger. To help you even more, it sends out a signal for your adrenal glands to produce the hormone cortisol. Cortisol activates fight or flight. This is good if your brain shuts down again after the danger has passed, but it's bad if it's never shut off.

Nowadays, we live in a world where we're always on high alert, not because there's imminent danger, but because we're being blasted by bad news 24/7 and our amygdala can't tell if something threatening is happening right behind us or halfway across the world. So the cortisol never stops flowing.

If this becomes chronic, it won't only take us down mentally, by burning out neural connections, but it will break down our immune systems, opening us up to physical diseases – anything from certain cancers and heart disease to type 2 diabetes and dementia.

How mindfulness works

When you become aware, your amygdala is activated. You'll know this because you'll be having frenzied thoughts. What you should do is intentionally take your focus to one of your senses: sound, sight, taste, touch or smell. When you sense any of these, a region in your brain called the insula will be activated. This area gives you a visceral awareness of your senses in contrast to you thinking about them.

You can calm down your amygdala by gently moving the focus to one of those senses activating your insula. You can't be in both regions or states at once – your thoughts are either churning, fuelled by cortisol, or you're in a mode of pure awareness with no thinking attached, bringing you a feeling of calm.

It's not so specifically amygdala vs insula – it's more lateral vs medial part of your brain. So when you're sending focus to your bodily senses, you're shifting activity away from your medial brain regions to your lateral brain regions.

Buffing up your brain

Mindfulness is a workout for your brain. There's no need to go to a gym; all the equipment you'll ever need is in your head. It's portable and always available.

The exercise of mindfulness is exactly like weight training; when you move from lying to sitting repeatedly, you're building an ab. When you focus your attention on a sense, notice when the thoughts come in and then bring your focus back to the sense. It's like doing a mental sit-up. Each mental sit-up builds more synaptic connections or white matter to your insula, which means it increases metacognition (the ability to stand back and watch your thoughts and feelings). The stronger your insula becomes, the easier it is to anchor your mind and quieten it down when being blasted by the high winds of stress.

A buff brain from practising mindfulness means you have more clarity of thought, instead of that frazzled feeling of one thought ramming into the next like a mental pile-up. In that state, it becomes impossible to remember anything, especially where you left your phone, which you're usually talking into.

This more lucid mind means more space for thoughts. This is when you can start thinking outside the box because the fear of failing has gone. So, now it gets fun. Now you can hit the creative zone called flow.

Without fear, you can fly.

Thoughts don't stop

The result of mindfulness practice isn't to stop thoughts (an impossibility unless you're dead, then you have an excuse) but to change your relationship to them. When you realise you can actually observe those insistent thoughts and quiet them down, you get the idea that thoughts aren't who you are. If thoughts *were* who you were, then how would you be able to watch them?

Our thoughts are storytellers making up narrative as they go, usually based on old memories playing randomly in our heads. They're a little more accurate when you're awake than when you're dreaming; when one minute you're a blowfish, the next you're ballroom dancing with Richard the Third, but they really are winging it as far as any connection to reality goes.

They're constantly changing without you even getting involved; if you wait a few seconds, a thought will pass and a new one will arise. Thoughts are transient, always coming and going at their own volition, like the weather. So when you're hit by a bombardment of those evil thoughts, you don't have to take them personally because *they* decide when to appear and disappear, not you. Think of them as a passing thunderstorm, suddenly followed by a blue sky, followed by high winds ... it just keeps coming without checking in with you. Or think of your thoughts like clouds passing, changing form from moment to moment.

And the mother of all *aha* moments is that thoughts aren't facts. That should lower your stress right there.

Pillar two: Stress reduction

Practising mindfulness isn't about getting it right. There's no right or wrong – no winner or loser. No one is marking your progress.

When you notice the thoughts have grabbed your attention again and again, you may assume it's because you're not doing the exercise correctly. Let me clear this up. For the exercise, you need the thoughts to pull you away to give you resistance. It would be like making the motion of lifting weights, with no weights. Don't think you can't do it because you're inept, your mind is too wild or it's too difficult. The more aggressive or volatile the thoughts, the better the workout and stronger your brain gets. Really fierce thoughts are the 30 kg weights and the light fluffy ones are the 0.5 kg weights.

Other regions of your brain can benefit from mindfulness

Each time you practise mindfulness, you're building up more density of white matter (more synaptic connections) and blood flow to your entire nervous system. This increases the blood flow to parts of your brain that help to regulate your emotions, such as your hippocampus, anterior cingulate cortex and lateral parts of your prefrontal cortex. Your heart rate slows, your respiration slows and your blood pressure drops.

A researcher from Harvard coined the changes in the body that meditation evokes as the "relaxation response" – basically the opposite to the "stress response". While the stress response is extremely detrimental to your body, the relaxation response is extremely salutary, and is probably at the root of the wide-ranging benefits that mindfulness has been found to have, both mentally and physically.

Your prefrontal cortex is involved with self-regulation and decision-making. It also enhances self-awareness and self-control, helping you to make constructive choices and let go of harmful ones.

Your anterior cingulate cortex is where you sense feelings, giving yourself an internal weather report. It's the centre of self-awareness and detects when your focus has moved from where you want it to be. It encircles your amygdala, so it can control distress and divert attention to somewhere else that's safer.

Your dorsolateral prefrontal cortex is an area that inhibits self-involvement, dampening down that self-obsessed, self-judging, self-critical mind. It's the region that helps you self-soothe and cover yourself in compassion.

So let's get those brain regions toughened up – get ready to give your mind a workout.

You don't need me to tell you but here are five of your senses, in case you're out of touch with yourself:

* ★ **taste**
* ★ **sound**
* ★ **touch**
* ★ **breath** (it's with mindfulness that we use breath as a sensation.)
* ★ **sight** – we aren't doing exercises involving sight because it's too tempting to get carried away by what you see.

Using curiosity to help you focus

Curiosity is the key to all of the exercises below. To not just fling your focus to a sense, but to investigate the subtlety of what something sounds/tastes/feels like. Part of the reason we're so easily distracted is that we (unlike kids) don't view something as if we're viewing it for the first time. We assume things have lost their novelty. We get bored easily . It's our eyes, ears, taste buds that are shut down.

These exercises aren't here to make you a better taster or listener, they're here to fine-tune your ability to pay attention because you can't pay attention to anything without curiosity.

Okay, now get off your ass and start the brain workout. Except you don't have to get off your ass, just stay on it, sitting down.

Remember: Nothing will change if you don't keep up the practice. You don't get a six pack by dreaming about one.

NB: Some of you have done these sense exercises with me before, either on one of my courses, or you've read them in *A Mindfulness Guide for the Frazzled*. Either way, they have to be delivered by rote, otherwise it's not mindfulness. It's like having to practise scales for the piano, tennis swings for tennis, or doing plie positions at the bar before you hit the stage and do *Swan Lake*. Repetition, repetition, repetition. The training is always the same – it's what you do with the training that makes the difference.

I've said it before, I'll say it again, because, hey, it's repetition … The first pillar of mindfulness is insight – noticing how your mind works. The second pillar is reducing stress. i.e. learning how to ground yourself by looking into your mind without being carried away or your mind getting out the whip.

Mindful exercises for stress reduction

Try doing one of these exercises once a day for five minutes.

Choose whichever time of the day is best. (I practise first thing in the morning when I get up.)

Exercise 1: Sense of taste

For this, you need a bite of food you like – your choice (mine is chocolate).

Stop: Notice what's going on in your mind? (Be honest – no one will ever find out, no matter how embarrassing it is.)

Taste: Put the chocolate or whatever you chose into your mouth, slow down and notice its:

★ flavour (salty, sweet, spicy, tangy, bland?)

★ texture (hard, soft, liquid, spiky, chewy?)

★ temperature (hot, cold, somewhere between the two?)

Take as long as you need to relish what you've put in your mouth.

Observe: Be aware of when your thoughts have drifted and begin to carry your focus away from the taste by commenting whether you like or don't like it, how fattening it is, wondering where the sock is you can't find, the call you need to make to explain why your Visa card has bounced, remembering where you left your sock, fantasising about winning the lottery, or whatever is running though your mind. (These are a few samples of my own random thoughts.)

Refocus: Once you notice your mind has gone off on a jag, take your focus back to the taste and savour the experience as if you might never taste food like this again.

Write down:

★ a few words of the sensations you remember

....

★ what this experience was like for you?

....

....

★ how it was different from normal eating?

....

....

The rewards of doing this mindfulness exercise are:

★ you've lowered your stress levels

★ food tastes a million times better when you slow it down and savour it

★ you'll probably lose weight from the usual style of eating, which would be wolfing it down

Exercise 2: Sound

Stop and notice: What's going on in your mind? What's the weather like? Stormy, sunny, hailing, breezy, etc. What are your thoughts?

Listen: Send your focus to whatever sound is going on around you. If you're listening to a bird, try to just hear its tweets and not think "bird". Try to notice the tone, volume, pitch and silence between the sounds.

Notice: Be aware of when your thoughts have started their usual parade of thinking in the past or future, fantasising, criticising, regretting, worrying, or you've just realised you weren't listening and you don't know where your mind went.

Refocus: Move your focus back to the sounds and tune in with curiosity.

Write down:

★ a few of the sounds you remember

....

....

★ what this experience was like for you?

....

....

....

★ how it was different from normal?

....

....

....

The rewards of doing this mindfulness exercise are:
★ you'll ground your wild and crazy brain
★ you'll notice sounds you've never noticed before, such as the wind, your breathing, more birds, silence...
★ you're exercising your ability to remain focused, even when the sounds are loud and disturbing

Exercise 3: Touch

Stop and notice: What's going on in your mind? Are your thoughts loud, quiet, nice, bitchy, rambling etc.?

Sense:
★ your feet on the floor (when sitting, standing or walking)
★ where your bum and backs of your thighs contact the chair or sofa you're sitting on
★ exactly where your body contacts the bed or sofa when you're lying down (good for helping you sleep)
★ holding something in your hand and noticing what it feels like in as much detail as possible

★ the wind on your skin

★ water on your skin (hot, cold, medium temperature)

Notice: Be aware of when other thoughts enter and pull your focus from where you felt those physical sensations.

Refocus: Gently take your focus from those thoughts back to wherever you felt the sensation.

Write down:

★ a few of the sensations you remember

....

....

....

★ what this experience was like for you?

....

....

....

★ how it was different from normal?

....

....

....

The rewards of doing this mindfulness exercise are:

★ you'll de-stress your brain

★ you'll feel more grounded, especially when you focus on your feet on the floor or bum on the chair – this usually gives a sense of being held and feeling safe

★ if you were lying down, you'll probably be asleep by now

Exercise 4: Breath

Stop: What are you thinking? Take your focus to your breath.

Breathe: Allow yourself to tune into where you feel yourself breathing through your nose or mouth and down into your lungs and back out again. Don't try to control your breath, just observe how your breath knows what to do without you interfering.

Notice: Be aware of when your thoughts pull you away on some mental slipstream.

Refocus: Gently take your focus back to your breathing. Really hone in on areas that you didn't notice before as far as the quality, depth and timing of each breath.

Write down:

★ a few words about the breath sensations you remember

....

....

....

★ what this experience was like for you?

....

....

....

★ how it was different to normal?

....

....

....

The rewards of doing this mindfulness exercise are:

★ you've calmed down

★ you're keeping yourself alive

★ you should feel more clear headed from all that fresh oxygen

After practising these short, easy sense exercises – which you can practise any time, anywhere, for a few minutes – you might like to learn a full mindfulness practice, which entails any combination of the above sensations.

You should do a variation of this exercise daily. You can begin by doing it for 10 minutes. Then, when you feel you're ready, increase the time to 20 or 30 or, dare I say, 40 minutes – up there with the big boys.

Mindfulness exercise – combination of touch, sound and breath

1   If you're sitting on a chair or sofa, move away from the back so your spine is self-supporting but not rigid, your head balanced on your neck but not held, your shoulders relaxed and your eyes open or closed.

2   Moving your attention as far from your gabbling mind as possible, take your focus to both of your feet and try to sense where they contact the floor.

3   Try to experience the feel of both feet from your toes to your heels, and side to side, feeling them rooted to the ground.

4   Let that focus go, and now move your attention to where you feel your body can sense contact with the chair or sofa. Feel the weight of your body and the effect of gravity pulling you down to the chair or sofa.

5   Let that focus go, and now take that spotlight of attention to sound. You don't have to go looking for the sound, let it come to you. Focus on what's coming in from the right side, the left side, above you, below you, in front of you, behind you.

6   Now, notice when you might start labelling the sounds or deciding which ones you like and don't like. Or when you don't even know where your mind has taken you, but you notice you're not listening anymore. Without berating yourself, or thinking you've done anything wrong (which you haven't, because all minds wander), escort your focus back to the sound.

7   Now let the sound fade into the background, bringing your focus to your breath. Notice where you feel your breath most vividly: the tip of your nose, mouth, chest, ribs or abdomen. In this area, just track as close as you can your inbreath and your outbreath and what happens between your inbreath and outbreath. Notice the depth, the speed, the texture of each breath and how different they are.

8   When the thoughts come in, as they always will, you can congratulate yourself for noticing and taking your focus back to the area where you were breathing. Don't try to control your breath – it knows what it's doing and can breathe without you having to do anything – so just sit back and experience the air show.

These exercises will give you stability when your mind gets agitated or scattered. Your breath is always there as an anchor to ground you.

If you don't have time or don't want to do a long sit, you can also choose to take mindful moments. Throughout the day wherever you are, whatever you're doing, check in for a few minutes or even one minute, to be able to give your brain a breather and come back to clarity and calm.

Mindfulness exercise: For the mindful minute

I wish I could find an acronym to make mindfulness easier to remember but I can't, so just tattoo these random letters onto yourself. **D G N R S**

D **Drop** your focus down into your mind and body and notice what's going on.

G **Ground** yourself by choosing a sense: your feet on the ground, your bum on the chair, sound or your breath.

N **Notice** when your thoughts start creeping in, taking you away from your focus.

R **Refocus** back to the sense you've chosen without giving yourself a hard time or judging yourself.
(This N (noticing of thoughts) and R (refocusing) is the back and forth of the exercise – there's no limit to how many times it happens in the time you've set.)

S **Stop**

If you only have 10 seconds free, just follow these instructions and come to your senses.

> Shine the light (inside)
> Be kind
> Shine the light
> Be kind
> Shine the light
> Be kind
> And so on...

Let me just reiterate why I'm giving you a crash course on mindfulness, because let's not kid ourselves, there have been so many books written about how it works, including mine called *Frazzled* (which, not being biased or anything, I highly recommend you should buy if you haven't already). The difference is, in this workbook, as promised, I'm going to help you deal with the Big Six because we've all had them up front and personal during lockdown. For over a year now, we've been bubbling away in a soup of existential angst while our kids screamed around us, our partners got sick of us. We were under threat of losing our jobs, and facing four walls wondering whether we were next on the ventilator.

Let's not pretend that there won't be some mental fallout from this, though there may be some people saying, "Oh good that's done with, now let's party." I don't think the mind can shake it off that quickly.

The thing that did almost as much damage as the pandemic during lockdown was the endless "what if" scenarios. We had to wait for the vaccine to stop the infection of Covid, but what could be done to help the accompanying mental anguish of constant worry and fear? I've given you these mindfulness exercises because it's what I happen to study, but it may not be for you. Hopefully, you've given it a try for longer than a few days. Just to remind you, nothing is easy in the beginning.

Some people say they practise mindfulness by running, listening to music, gardening etc. These activities are good for you; they're relaxing or they give you a great workout and endorphin-high but they aren't giving you the same benefits as mindfulness exercises. Those brain regions developed through mindfulness for greater insight, focus, stress control and compassion can only be exercised by moving your focus from a physical sensation to your thoughts and from your thoughts back to the physical sensation.

Other activities, such as tai chi, qigong, yoga, pilates and certain martial arts, are also mindfulness practices, in that they involve moving your focus back and forth between your mind and body. It's the back and forth between your mind and body that makes the difference.

Pillar three: Emotional awareness

Congratulations for getting this far in this workbook. If you just opened it up here, then welcome. I'll fill you in on what you missed. We've practised mindfulness for pillar one – insight – how to observe your thoughts without getting caught in them. We've done exercises for pillar two – stress reduction – lowering our stress levels and getting our mind steady. And now we move to the next pillar – emotional awareness.

Being aware of our emotions

What we need to do is what we've probably been avoiding our whole lives: drop down into our bodies and face those disturbing emotions that we might as well imagine as monsters. As the saying goes, "Run away from them, they'll chase you. Face them, and they run from you."

It seems counterintuitive to face something that's upsetting, but awareness of these disturbing emotions means they won't suddenly erupt when you least expect and potentially ruin relationships, your work or your mental wellbeing. No question we all love to jump into the emotional pool when everything's fine and the water's warm. Everyone loves feeling that burst of joy – those tingling fireworks in the heart.

But the problem is we don't live in those waters all the time. So when it begins to boil, the practice of mindfulness is what keeps us swimming and not sinking (and getting fried). It isn't some spiritual bypass and a one-way ticket to bliss. It's, as I've said, a mental workout to be able to keep your equilibrium no matter what's thrown at you – whether it's the good, the bad or the ugly.

If we want to get to know our emotions, we have to go via our bodies because that's where they live. Unless we become aware of our emotions, just like thoughts, they'll drag us from one state to the next until we frazzle on that roller coaster we can't stop. Also, like recognising our habits of thinking, only when we're aware of our emotional habits can we begin to unpick the locks that keep us shackled to them.

I'm going to give you mindfulness exercises to be able to navigate around those emotional hijacks and ultimately find freedom in spite of their intensity. Before we can start to focus on emotions, we need to get acquainted with the terrain they live in – our body. It's time to become aware of this larger continent of us down there.

The first pillar of mindfulness – insight – is how we become aware of our thoughts. But awareness of the feelings in your body is almost more crucial. We only think a thought 200 milliseconds after we experience a bodily sensation. This is probably because language came online (about 150,000 years ago) after we'd already existed for around five and a half million years. If we had to wait those millions of years for language to be developed while we were being chased by a wild predator, where would we be? Not here.

Evolution in its brilliance gave us a warning system that didn't need words because there weren't any. We didn't have to wait to hear "run" in our heads. Our bodies got us the hell out of there.

We've gradually lost touch with our bodies since talking started. It's supposed to be more socially acceptable than just hitting someone over the head if you don't agree with them.

We always talk about our emotions, but thoughts aren't accurate translators of feelings. What we think might be heartache might just be heartburn – who knows? So many blues songs have been written about what could have just been indigestion. Luckily, people like Billie Holiday didn't know that, or it would have depressed her even more.

Anyway, we need this pillar to be able to tune into – and become aware of – what our body is experiencing, not through words but through sensations. This is "emotional insight".

We all know our bodies from the outside after years of sucking in our stomachs at the mirror, noting every new crevice, crinkle, cellulite dimple, hair gain or hair loss. We tone, buff and rub scent and moisturiser onto them, mainly to find a mate. (Baboons bend over – we buff.)

We usually don't pay much attention to our insides, unless our attention is alerted to a jab of pain or a jab of sex. We aren't even aware of our bodies when we're working out – we go through the motions, crunches, kicks, pumping weights and stretches on autopilot, either to look better or feel healthier (no doubt – exercise is good for you). But outside of that, outside of the gym, we mainly think of our bodies as supermarket trolleys that wheel our brains from one location to the next.

So before we visit our emotions, I'm going to do a body scan that you can practise as a way of saying "Hi" to your inner landscape. A tune-in to sensations down below.

Emotional awareness exercises

How to do a body scan

Focus into each area I mention with a sense of curious investigation as if your body is under the microscope of a brilliant scientist (you).

1 Sitting on a chair or sofa, make sure your spine is self-supporting.

2 Focusing from the bottom of your spine, feeling each vertebra (the bones in your spine) stacked one on top of the next – balanced, not rigid.

3 Feel your head lightly balanced on the top of your neck and let your shoulders fall and relax.

4 Your feet should both be flat on the ground. Begin by moving your focus to where you feel them make contact with the floor, from your toes to your heels, and side to side. Try and sense the footprint of both of your feet on the floor.

5 Let that sensation dissolve and move your focus up your legs, including your knees. Feel your skin outside and your bones and muscles inside.

6 Now, moving your focus up the thighs, feeling their weight on the back of the chair and their circumference and everything you can sense inside of them.

7 Let that focus fade and bring it to your pelvis. Sense how it's pushing down on the chair – the weight of it.

8 Now bring your focus from your right hip bone to your left and everything in between. Notice if there are any sensations of discomfort. Are they pulsing, stabbing, loose or tight? Or are they neutral?

9 Leave that area of your focus and bring it up from your waist to your neck, taking in the back of your body, the sides and up the front – your whole torso. Pay attention to all sensations in this area, the movement of your breath, your lungs expanding and contracting, your heart beating and your blood flowing.

10 Let your attention leave that area and bring it to both hands and where you feel them making contact on your lap or clasped together. Sensing each finger and between each finger, up both arms, your elbows and to your shoulders. Feeling the weight of both arms hanging from your shoulders.

11 Let go of your arms and move your attention into your neck, noticing the position you're holding it or if it's tight or loose.

12 Let that image go and move to your jaw, noticing if it's rigid or relaxed.

13 And now, one at a time, move the focus of your awareness to your lips, tongue, nose, cheeks, eye sockets, eyelids, eyebrows, forehead and the top of your head.

14 You've pulled awareness to each area and honed in on the sensations. Now, widen your lens of attention to your entire body, from your toes to the top of your head, including your arms, and sense the breath filling your whole body and leaving it. Notice the speed and depth and how different each breath is from the next. Notice what happens between your inbreath and outbreath.

15 Sit back and just observe. If thoughts come, escort them back to the awareness of your whole body breathing.

Okay, now stop.

Exercise

★ Write down which areas of your body you were more aware of than others.

....

....

....

....

....

....

★ Write down which sensations you noticed in those areas.

....

....

....

....

....

....

★ Were there areas where you felt nothing or felt numb?

....

....

....

....

....

....

You don't have to sit still, in one place, to tune into your body. You can do it anywhere, at any time.

Here are some suggestions.
★ Sense the wind on your face.
★ Sense the experience of showering on your skin – temperature, pressure, texture.
★ Focus on the sensations in your hands, arms and back when you're holding or lifting something.
★ Tuning into the sensations in your muscles when exercising, walking or performing any chore.
★ Sense your fingertips on the keys while you're typing (I'm doing it now).

Make up your own:

....

....

....

....

....

....

....

....

So now you're aware of what's under your skin, let's move into those murkier waters where your emotions live up close and personal.

Exercise: "Sensing your emotions"

Below is a list of emotions. Next to each is an outline of a body. Send your focus to where you feel those emotions inside. Feel free to add your own.

Now draw exactly where you feel the sensation of each emotion in your body. What's the shape of its boundaries? A circle? Jagged or straight lines?

Shade in the area to represent how heavy or light your emotions feel.

Write beside the drawing a list of what the sensations were like, i.e. twinging, pulsing, stabbing, numbness, coldness, heat etc.

Sadness

....

....

....

....

....

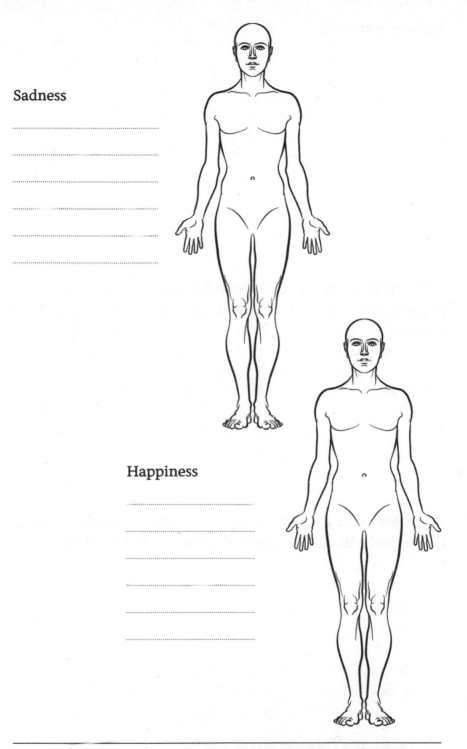

Happiness

....

....

....

....

....

....

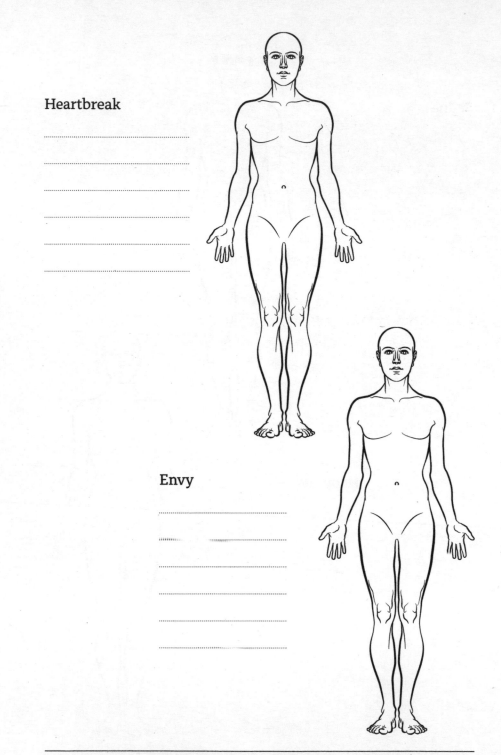

Heartbreak

....

....

....

....

....

....

Envy

....

....

....

....

....

....

Love

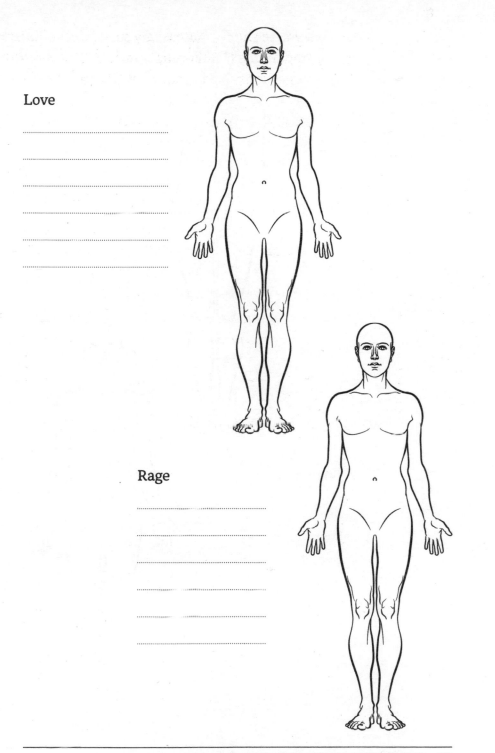

....

....

....

....

....

Rage

....

....

....

....

....

....

Fear

....

....

....

....

....

....

Shame

....

....

....

....

....

....

Every time we're caught out by an emotion that we aren't aware of, we're immediately imprisoned by the habitual way we react to it. We might feel a general hurt, but then we add on our own layer of pain, thinking, "It's all my fault and I'm useless." This might lead to depression (my way). Or something makes us angry and we think, "Everyone is always letting me down" (also my way). We add these layers without any awareness that we're doing it and assume it's as real as the original feeling. Jon Kabat-Zinn (my hero) always says, "Pain is pain but suffering is optional."

When you can sit back and observe the sensations, rather than mentally beating yourself up about them, you're stepping back from the emotions and giving them space so you get that "this too shall pass" vibe. With this distancing, you're taking the heat off by paradoxically tuning into the bare sensations rather than examining the "whys" and "wherefores".

You won't automatically snap out of your upsetting emotions and skip through fields, but you'll give yourself space to take the burn off and think with clarity how to respond. The more you practise, the faster you get at identifying and ultimately freeing yourself from the sting of negative emotions.

Pillar four: Presence

If you're thinking, "What's she talking about? Of course I'm present. I'm here, aren't I? Somebody is wearing my clothes and I assume it's me," my answer is, "Your body may well be where you're sitting, but your mind is probably out of town." James Joyce writes, in his book *Dubliners*, "Mr Duffy lived a short distance from his body." And we all understand what that means.

On average, we spend about 28% of our lives planning, 33% reminiscing and 48% mind-wandering, which means you've got about 1% left for right now.

Mark Williams, co-creator of mindfulness-based cognitive therapy (and, more importantly, my professor), writes, "If you are 30 years old, with a life expectancy of around 80, you have 50 years left. But if you are only truly conscious and aware of every moment for perhaps two out of 16 hours a day, your life expectancy is only another six years and three months. If a friend told you they had just been diagnosed with a terminal disease that will kill them in six years, you would be filled with grief and try to comfort them. Yet without realising it, you may be daydreaming along such a path yourself. If you could double the number of hours that you were truly alive each day, then, in effect, you would be doubling your life expectancy. It would be like living to 130."

To become present, you don't have to go into some enlightened "eyes rolled to the back of the head" state. We've all experienced being present at some point when we're suddenly riveted by that rainbow or when a seagull lands on our head. Both of these are "aha" moments, unless the seagull decides to use you as a loo, then it's not so "aha".

With mindfulness, the controls are yours to decide when you want to go into present mode or not. This means you could spend longer being aware and awake in your life than not. I think that might be the deal of the century. I don't mean awake as in not sleeping, I mean switched on to things you've never noticed before when you were on autopilot. Now almost anything can be an "aha". You're breathing and alive, that's pretty "aha" right there.

The reason we don't often visit the present is because our minds are usually too busy whacking back and forth between the past and future. We have the ability to mentally time travel for the sake of our survival. We can go back to our past to remember tactics that worked or didn't work to picture success in the future.

Your **body** may well be where you're sitting, but your **mind** is probably elsewhere

Our other gift is that we can go on autopilot. This was a time saver so we don't have to think while walking, "Move left leg forwards, lift right hip, kick right leg forwards." Walking without thinking was a great success so we applied autopilot to most of our current activities.

We spend so much of our lives worrying about the future, but whatever it brings, it won't be what we expect. And when it finally comes, it will be "now", too. We miss so many moments of this limited life by being overly preoccupied with things that haven't happened yet.

This isn't to say we should stop recalling the past or planning for the future. Without those capabilities we wouldn't survive, but the problem is that that's all we do – always missing what's going on right in front of us.

With mindfulness, you're training your mind to focus where you want it to focus, and that includes focusing it on the present moment. That can only happen when your mind is calm (and your amygdala is switched off).

The reason for past and future thinking is because you're on high alert (your amygdala is switched on). Your mind is flicking to the past to figure out what you already did that worked or didn't work to ensure a successful outcome in the future.

Even on holiday, we're planning for the next one or comparing it to a past one. (Sometimes when I'm on holiday, even if it's perfect, I miss the whole thing because I'm sitting there swiping through Airbnbs around the world and checking their availability.)

I read this on a postcard somewhere: "Having a great time. Wish I was here."

Here's another saying about the present: "Wherever you go, there you are. Your luggage is another story."

I don't want to give the impression that we should immediately pack our bags and move into the "now", where we'd all be so "chilled" and "vegged out'" that nothing would get done. That would mean not only would *you* never accomplish anything, but *no one* would be motivated to fight the good fight for climate change, human rights or world peace. That means it would be in the hands of the politicians and then we'd all be screwed.

I love how Jon Kabat-Zinn talks about the future. He says (I've paraphrased a tiny bit), "Now is the future of the previous moment just past, and the future of all those moments that were before that one ... When we are mindful of now, no matter what we are doing or saying or working on or experiencing, the next moment is influenced by our presence of mind, and is thus different from how it would have been, had we not been paying attention, had we not been caught up in some whirlpool or other within the mind or body. So if we wish to take care of the now, the only way we can do that is to take care of the future of all past moments and efforts, i.e. recognise each moment as a branch point and realise that what we decide to do at each of these branch points makes all the difference to how our one wild and precious life will unfold. *We take care of the future best by taking care of the present now.*"

Becoming present is implicit in all mindfulness exercises. Whenever you're focusing on any of the five senses, it always

---

means you're present, because you can't hear a sound from yesterday or tomorrow. It's always "now". The stressy thoughts have quietened down, and the only things incoming are moment-by-moment sensations of your skin, through your eyes, ears, nose and mouth. Some call it "the present of all presents".

A few times while practising, I've had an "aha" moment, where suddenly the hamster wheel of worry about the future and re-runs of the past jerks to a stop. All is still and quiet with a backdrop of the hallelujah of being alive. It feels like a cat is purring in my heart and sunlight is moving through my veins. This is when I recognise I'm happy. It makes the years of practising mindfulness worth it. It's as dazzling as Eckhart Tolle says it is – this sense of being in the "now".

All the same, I've been taught not to try to hold on to that state or recreate it, because then you're back to square one, chasing and craving the next buzz. That's when the stress starts cooking and the thoughts start churning. That "aha" will happen again when *it* decides to make an appearance, not you.

Presence with others

As wonderful as the "aha" is, it isn't the point of practising mindfulness. You're building up muscle so that your own thoughts have taken a back seat and the red fog of confusion has lifted. Now there's space in your mind to pay attention to what other people are trying to say below their words. You can pick up what they're genuinely feeling and what it's like to be in their shoes.

I think you can only show this kind of empathic attention when your mind is settled. Thoughts still come and go but they won't carry your focus away from the other person. People are at their happiest when they feel they're being heard and someone cares, so you're using your presence as the ultimate present. No need to buy people candles anymore to show you care – just turn up and listen deeply to them.

Outside of formal mindfulness exercise, you can practise becoming instantly present by bringing focus to a sense anywhere, at any time.

Exercise

Become present instantly by focusing on:
★ the sensation of your breathing
★ tasting what's in your mouth
★ smelling lilac, bread, drains, food...
★ hearing birds, drilling, music, silence, shouting, laughing...
★ feeling anything on your skin

If you want to experience these senses all at once and really get a hit of presence, take a walk with awareness – it will change your life.

Mindful walking

Try not to have a destination when you're walking so there's no rush. Set yourself a time (20 minutes a day if you can manage it).

You know how to walk – I don't need to give you instructions – but the idea is to walk mindfully.

Don't do all these suggestions at once, or you'll flood your brain with too much choice. Choose a few suggestions for each walk and enjoy it.

Here are some suggestions:

★ Notice your feet as they contact the ground.
★ Feel the movements from inside your legs, torso, shoulders, arms.
★ Notice what expression your facial muscles are making.
★ Soak in sounds, smells and sights around you – intentionally focus on things you've never noticed before, i.e. tops of the trees, the sky, insects, details of leaves, the way other people walk, how they're dressed.
★ Focus on your emotions and breathing.

Make up your own:

....

....

....

....

....

....

....

....

....

....

Exercise

Write down whether you noticed:

- ★ sounds
- ★ sights
- ★ smells
- ★ sensations in your body
- ★ new things you never noticed before

....

....

....

....

....

....

....

....

If you feel inclined, feel free to pick up your pencil, pen or crayon and draw what you saw and want to remember. It's not an art class so any doodle or scribble is perfect.

Pillar five: Kindness or compassion

Without this ingredient, you're not doing mindfulness, no matter how much you practise. When you're focusing on what's going on in your mind or body and you don't use kindness, you'll just beat yourself up more because, as we all know, it's not a happy, all-singing, all-dancing musical playing inside you all the time.

When you notice the inevitable thoughts sweeping you away for the thousandth time, you'll more likely than not pile on the cruelty for not being able to control them or for hating what they're telling you. The only antidote for this self-whipping is kindness, which, like every other skill we've practised so far, can be developed or strengthened.

I think this is a perfect description of self-compassion: "If you're shot with an arrow, you just pull it out. It doesn't help to worry about who shot it, why they shot it and whether they'll shoot it again. Just take it out."

We might have been born with kindness, and probably were, but life's pressure cooker may have boiled it away.

When a mother cradles her baby, she exudes a chemical called oxytocin that soothes her baby and calms it down. Eventually, with this consistent early training, her baby learns to self-soothe for later in life, just like Mommy taught it when it feels frightened.

If your parents failed at soothing you, either because they didn't read the instructions or were out to lunch, like mine were, then you might feel, like I've felt throughout my life, as if you were dropped from the sky and no one was there to catch you.

Practising mindfulness makes up for Mommy (thank God). For me, it's true that when my triggers are being hit fast and furiously, I can, not necessarily skip with joy, but somewhat cool down my cortisol and swerve from an oncoming depression. I feel every emotion known to man on a regular basis, but they're not taking me down like they used to.

Showing kindness to others

When you bring in compassion or kindness, you're not going gooey, giving yourself a yummy, steamy hot cocoa while luxuriating in warm yak milk. You're practising it on yourself to be able to take it to other people. It's the same with presence; you can only be present for other people if you're present in yourself.

If you can switch on your own oxytocin, which comes on automatically when you're self-soothing, you can soothe others. If you're aware of how agonising thoughts and emotions can be inside you and then see someone going ten out of ten on the hissy-fit frontier, you'll recognise it's because it feels like hell inside of them, too, and they're only trying to get it out. It's nothing personal, it's because it's intolerable.

If we don't realise that someone is suffering exactly the same way we are, we'll send back an artillery of retaliation, raging at them for causing us pain. Then it accelerates to war. On the other hand, if you're aware that the other person is in exactly the same pain as you are, you should bring compassion into the ring.

We can spend the rest of our lives blaming and brooding about how someone dumped on us and then justify dumping on them in return. If we don't start using kindness on ourselves and the other person, nothing will change.

We've all spewed out our angst, thinking it will give us some relief, and look what's happened? What a contribution to the world. That's why it's in trouble. We need to save ourselves first by throwing ourselves a compassion-bone, and then go out and try to save the world.

It's easier than you think. You don't have to go back to school and retrain. You don't even have to dig into your past and forgive everyone for screwing you up.

All you have to do is redecorate your inner world or closet. (Remember the closet metaphor I used many moons ago at the start of this workbook? Well, it's back.)

Find the "on" button to start your oxytocin flowing. That can be done by simply doing an act of kindness. Once that juice is cascading through you, spread it out to the world and bathe in it yourself.

Even if you're turning it on just to improve your health as an antidote for stress, it doesn't matter. Just doing the act (fake it till you make it) changes everything for the better.

Exercise 1

Write a list of things you can do to get a hit of that oxytocin.

Here are my suggestions:
- ★ Go to an old people's home and say hi to everyone.
- ★ Smile at someone you pass in the street who looks sad.
- ★ Send a postcard to kids in a hospital.
- ★ Make a "thank you" package for the rubbish collector or post-person.
- ★ Go up to someone who works for the NHS and thank them.

Now it's your turn:

1 ....

2 ....

3 ....

4 ....

5 ....

6 ....

7 ....

8 ....

If you're short on ideas, my son Max has an app called dropkindnessnotbombs.com and has over 200 acts of kindness suggestions – a mother likes to push.

Another oxytocin-maker is writing a list of things you're grateful for.

Exercise 2

Try to write at least five things a week you're grateful for.

Here are mine:
- ★ At this moment, I don't have pain in my body.
- ★ At this moment, I don't have depression.
- ★ I have kids who are happy.
- ★ I can make a living by writing.
- ★ I can be funny.

Now do your own:

1 ....
2 ....
3 ....
4 ....
5 ....
6 ....
7 ....
8 ....

Using this workbook and practising the exercises is another act of kindness. You've cooled down your overagitated mind by giving it a place to rest. Aren't you glad you bought this workbook? And everyone around you should thank you for buying it too, because kindness is contagious – like a positive virus that everyone around you catches. I always call this neural Wi-Fi.

If we don't **start** using kindness on ourselves and the **other** person, nothing will change

Mindfulness for the Big Six realities

We've been through the five pillars of mindfulness but, as promised, I'm going to show you how to apply them to the Big Six. We don't have to wait for them to strike – they are as omnipresent as the weather.

I'm going to go through each of the six realities with mindfulness exercises to help you create a strong anchor to hold onto the next time the storms of uncertainty, change, loneliness, dissatisfaction and death try to blow your mind, while applying insight, lowering stress, and increasing emotional awareness, presence and kindness.

Reality check one: Difficult emotions

We only think of these emotions as difficult because they don't feel good. But emotions, good and bad, are not only what make us human, they're the reason we've survived this far. Evolution provided them on purpose to give us the basics – from avoiding what's unpleasant and dangerous or potentially fatal – to being attracted to what's pleasurable and safe, like food and sex (to make sure we stick around long enough to breed an all-new version of us).

That's all nature asks of us. It doesn't care where we bought our clothes, or what we do for a living, it just wants us to not die until we've made another human. All emotions have a reason, but how to live with the more-difficult ones is where this practice comes in handy.

So rather than kick ourselves harder when we feel the torrent of fear, anger and panic, we need to learn to live peacefully beside them, even going so far as to thank them for getting us this far. Okay, maybe not thanking them, but at least acknowledging they have – or had – a purpose outside making us miserable.

The following poem, "The Guesthouse" by Rumi, is used by many mindfulness teachers to encourage us to be open to all our emotions. Not just the fun ones.

> This being human is a guesthouse. Every morning a new
>   arrival.
> A joy, a depression, a meanness, some momentary
>   awareness comes as an unexpected visitor.
> Welcome and entertain them all! Even if they're a crowd
>   of sorrows, who violently sweep your house empty of
>   its furniture.
> Still, treat each guest honorably. He may be cleaning you
>   out for some new delight.
> The dark thought, the shame, the malice. Meet them at
>   the door laughing, and invite them in.
> Be grateful for whoever comes, because each has been
>   sent as a guide from beyond.

Exercises for difficult emotions

Exercise 1:

Write down your most difficult emotion. Beside it, write specifically what it brings up in you, and why.

These are mine:

★ **Fear of getting found out.** My parents contributed to this feeling by taking me to doctors when I was young, after failing in all subjects at school, to check if there was something wrong with my brain. Ever since, I've been expecting a bad result.

★ **Envy.** Hating when someone gets a job I want, or don't even want (I just don't want anyone else to have it). My daughters celebrate when their friends do well. I don't understand where they got this gene.

★ **Anger.** Earlier, I wrote that I was in the habit of finding someone who made a mistake or made me feel as if I had made a mistake, and then continuously punishing them for it. I couldn't turn off that rage valve. This was a gift from my father, who lived for revenge. He went back to Austria after the Nazis kicked him out and, 30 years later, identified who his tormentors were and wouldn't leave until they were all jailed.

★ **Heartbreak.** Everybody is having the time of their lives and I wasn't invited. A leftover from childhood.

★ **Shame.** When I feel shame, here's what comes to my mind: see all of the above. I'm ashamed about how pathetically petty my negative emotions are. I'm a healthy, privileged person, so feeling those things when other people are really suffering makes me feel like a wanker.

Write down yours:

1

2

3

4

5

Exercise 2:

Write down who or what or where brings up feelings of kindness or compassion.

Here are mine:

★ Sox (my cat)

★ walking in a forest with bird sounds

★ my kids

★ swimming or standing in a warm swimming pool

★ eating nuts while watching Netflix

Now write down yours

1 ....

2 ....

3 ....

4 ....

5 ....

6 ....

7 ....

8 ....

Mindfulness exercise: adding kindness to difficult emotions

A reminder that, from now on, each mindfulness exercise in this workbook will include the five pillars – that's why we practised them. These pillars are:

> **insight**
> **stress reduction/grounding yourself**
> **emotional awareness**
> **presence**
> **kindness**

Exercise

Sitting up in a position of wakefulness, your head balanced on the top of your neck, with your shoulders down.

D: **Drop** your attention into your mind and notice the internal weather condition. Stormy? Sunny with a light breeze? Snowy?

G: **Ground** yourself by focusing on the sensations of your feet contacting the ground, your bum and back of your thighs contacting the seat, feeling supported and held so your body can let go of muscle tension and relax. Now move your focus to the sound around you and/or your breath.

N: **Notice** when the thoughts grab your attention away from the senses of touch, sound or breath.

R: In this more present state, observe thoughts coming and going, then gently **refocus** back to a sense. Bring to mind one of your difficult emotions that you wrote down, and notice how it feels in your body.

Sense the edges, the size and accompanying sensations. Throbbing? Numb? Stabbing? Hot? Cold?

G: Let go of the sensations and **ground** yourself again by sensing your body, sound and/or breath.

Now when you're ready, bring in a word from the list of positive images and words. Feed them in slowly and notice how they feel in your body: location, edges and textures.

N: Notice when the thoughts enter to explain what's going on or wherever else they take you.

R: Refocus back to the feelings associated with the positive images.

As an experiment, try putting your hand over your heart and experiencing whatever comes up, as you breathe into and out of that area against your hand. You could also try gently turning the ends of your mouth up, so you're slightly smiling. Try not to look for a result, just notice it.

S: Okay, now **stop**.

Write down the difficult emotion you chose.

....

....

Below is an outline of a body. Draw where the difficult emotion was in your body. Ideally with a crayon to show the specific colour of the sensation.

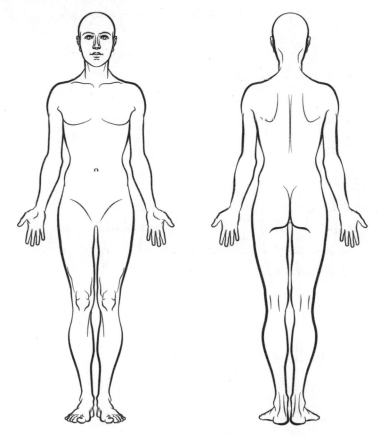

Now write down the soothing word or image you choose.

....

....

....

....

....

....

Draw into the same outline of the body where you experienced the soothing emotion in your body.

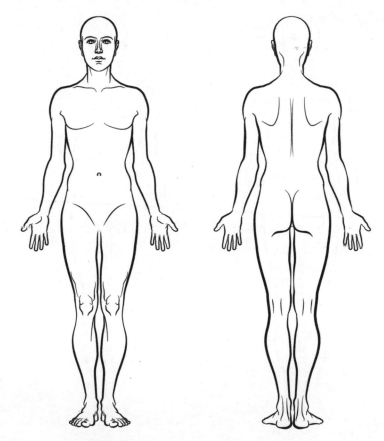

Write what it felt like to have both the difficult and the positive sensations.

....

....

....

....

....

....

Did one override the others and, if so, which one?

....

....

....

....

....

....

As the exercise went on, did one of them – or both – disperse, changing locations or textures?

....

....

....

....

....

....

What did it feel like when you put your hand on your heart?

....

....

....

....

....

What did it feel like to smile?

....

....

....

....

....

....

Exercises for difficult emotions around others

As I previously mentioned, when a difficult emotion has stabbed us in the heart or gut or wherever we feel the pain, our tendency is to project our feelings onto other people. We should also give kindness to those who are hurling their emotions at us (probably for the same reason we do) to get rid of the pain. Bringing kindness to the situation could nip a potential screaming match in the bud.

Try these kindness techniques – you'll both feel better.

Exercise 1

If you find yourself in a confrontational situation where someone is giving you hell, excuse yourself. Politely tell the person who's being abusive that you need to attend to something important and you'll be right back. (This is a lie but sometimes you have to do what you have to do.)

Things to do to cool down once you've left:

⭐ If you have time, go for a five-minute walk (Be careful – if you're gone too long, they'll get even more pissed off).

⭐ Look at an image of something that makes you feel good: a holiday snap, your dog, hamster, partner, Deliveroo menu.

⭐ Do some mindfulness in the loo.

Then go back.

Exercise 2

Staying where you are when someone is giving you grief.

★ Ground yourself to lower your hot emotions by sending focus to your breathing.

★ Try to delicately tip the person off-balance by bringing in some kindness when it's least expected. For example, tell them you like their tie, ask how their kids are or where they like to go on holiday. (Do this with subtlety or else they'll think you've lost your mind.)

★ By now you should know that when you focus on a sense, your cortisol levels lower. We haven't used sight before, but we will now. While the person is berating you, focus on their left or right nostril. Or left or right eyebrow. The choice is yours. Investigate those areas with curiosity, noticing the colour, shape and texture. They'll think you're listening and are fascinated by what they're saying. Using the sense of sight, anchor your anger – and once you're calm, they'll calm down. You might notice it's worked because now they're staring at *your* left nostril.

Taking care of yourself after the incident:

★ Be aware that after someone has given you a hard time, the memory of it lives on. Your thoughts will be dying to rehash the incident so you can revisit the adrenaline kick that anger produces.

★ Beware of the temptation to tell everyone you know about the incident because it will only churn up your rage.

Exercise on labelling emotions:
Name it to tame it

This exercise is about labelling the emotional changes when you experience them. Don't think too much about what the label is – just choose whatever word seems relevant. When you label an emotion, a space opens up around the feeling, and the intensity of the emotion lowers. You're stepping back from the feeling and becoming an observer of it. You can repeat the word as long as the sensation stays and, if the emotion changes, give it a new label.

Researchers from UCLA found that when people become aware of their emotions and label them, i.e. anger and label it as "anger", the part of the brain that generates negative emotions, the amygdala, calms down. It's almost as if once the emotional message has been delivered to the conscious mind, it can quieten down a little.

The labelling disidentifies your hot emotions, changing your relationship to your thoughts. If your thoughts and feelings have labels, they're no longer some solid part of you. Instead, they're transient items that come and go at random. It's as if you're saying, "Oh, that's anxiety," rather than "I'm anxious".

When you label an **emotion**,
the **intensity** of the
emotion is reduced

Mindfulness exercise for labelling

Sitting in a chair.

G: Sense your feet grounding you to the floor, your bum on the seat, your body feeling held and relaxed.

N: Notice your breath coming into your body through your nose or mouth, filling your lungs and exiting in its own time, without trying to control it.

N: Notice when your thoughts begin to take your attention, and tune into them. As your thoughts come in, and as soon as you recognise where the story is going, see if you can identify it. You might notice your thinking is about planning for something in the future – if so, say to yourself "planning". When the thoughts begin their story about something fearful in the future, label it by saying, "worrying", "futuring" or "fear". If you notice you're regretting something you've done, think "regret" and so on...

R: When the thoughts become too strong, bring your focus back to the sense of sitting and breathing.

S: Okay, now stop.

The earlier you catch an old thought pattern coming down the pipeline, the less likely those negative thoughts will take root and drag you away from being in the present. Remember to be kind whenever your mind drifts.

Reality check two: Uncertainty

We humans live in a comfort zone of believing that things are "same old, same old" (thus the expression). Did we think before the pandemic that everything was certain? Was everyone a psychic and they just weren't telling me?

The fact is, the world can turn on a dime and events are beyond our control. You can wake up one morning and the horror show you've been dreaming about the night before is suddenly the new normal. Now you know what the dinosaurs must have felt like – one moment, they were minding their own business grazing, and the next ... BANG! One meteorite hits, and they're dust. See what I mean about uncertainty? No one saw it coming.

We can't deal with uncertainty, and we don't want to, but at some point we have to wake up and face the music.

This is a good moment to wise up to the fact that because we never know what's coming, we might as well enjoy our lives while we're still living them. The faster we make friends with the certainty of uncertainty, the freer and happier we'll be.

No matter how hard you study, invest, sacrifice, promise and commit, your future is out of your hands. I'm not implying you shouldn't bother making plans or envisioning the future, because there's no progress without a plan. I'm saying, when your predictions don't happen, don't punish yourself. Nobody can know the future.

Surprise!!!

If there was no uncertainty, the word "surprise" wouldn't exist. If you take surprise or uncertainty away, our existence would be a constant beige.

Surprise is how you get your first big hit of adrenaline – when Mummy or Daddy or a caregiver go "peekaboo" or play jack-in-the-box! That's your first taste of the explosive feeling of the unexpected which, in positive situations, turns to laughter. Laughing is actually a combination of shock and relief, so your hands go over your mouth to stifle a potential scream. Then, when we realise what we expected to happen hasn't happened, the relief causes a sudden exhalation and sounds like a seal barking, which we call a laugh. Laughing comes with the high of an endorphin rush, and that's what comedians are paid for – to deliver that hit of endorphins.

Mindfulness exercise for uncertainty

Write down a time in your life when you were at a crossroads. Then think about these situations and what you thought would happen next:

1   when you finished secondary school or high school
2   when you got your first job
3   when you got married or moved in with a significant partner
4   after you had kids (if you have)
5   after the lockdown was over

Now write beside each of these, what actually happened?

Reality check three: Loneliness

We struggled with loneliness long before lockdown. We pretended to be part of one big happy electronic family by zinging back and forth a few emojis, but that's still loneliness. One of the problems is we're so "avalanched" under notifications and emails piling up, waiting to be dealt with, that we've stopped being able to differentiate between which ones are work, family, friends or spam. They all need answering, and they all need answering now. No wonder we can't breathe.

Responding to any email or WhatsApp or text or pigeon dropping a letter to you from the sky has become a chore. The dream of dreams is that we don't have to respond to even one more demand from the snowslide of requests. The relief when someone I've made arrangements to meet cancels is beyond words. I do a little "they've cancelled" dance, even when it's someone I love or couldn't wait to see (even my kids, for God's sake). I pretend to be annoyed, but inside I'm thinking, "Whoopee, I'm free to stay in and catch up with more emails." How sad is that? And no wonder WhatsApp took off, because you can't cram in long responses in such a little box. Just send a heart, that's good enough to show you're still alive and care, even if you've just sent that to your plumber, which I often do, because my hand is on automatic.

While I'm on the topic of my loneliness, I might as well tell you about how I experience it, because it's been my constant companion throughout my life. Loneliness has motivated all my decisions and shaped who I've become, because I was always alone when I was young. I thought the reason no one liked me was because my parents were weird and, clearly, I was a carrier of that weirdness and no one wanted to catch it.

Every day, since childhood, my main motive has been to be accepted, to ensure I wouldn't have to be alone. And certainly not alone with my parents in the house we lived in, which was overwhelmingly frightening. I made desperate attempts to glue myself onto gangs or cliques in high school, but was always rejected. It didn't help that my father nicknamed me "sad sack", which means loser in any language.

I lived isolated, except for a few fellow weirdo strays. We'd roam the high-school halls looking for a group to hang with. We tried to hang out with each other, but it was useless – we were all too creepy and desperate so we broke up.

Then, around 16, a miracle happened. I don't recall how it happened, but I saw Joan Rivers on television and within 24 hours, I had turned myself from a loser into America's hottest comedian, actress, writer, producer and television host all in one. I was suddenly channelling Joan Rivers and, beyond my control, her lines were coming out of my mouth. Overnight, I was doing stand-up in front of the boys and became the alternative prom queen (still weird, but I made weird fashionable). Most of my fanbase were homosexuals, but who cared?

I could never switch "Joan" on in front of my parents, as they had locked me into the label of "sad sack". But outside of the house, I was going full Vegas at parties, in the playground, in the loo. I became her, though strangely when I met Joan Rivers later in my life, not even Joan was Joan – she was vulnerable, a little jittery and unsure of herself. A made-up person, just like me.

By the end of high school, my parents were taking me to career counsellors, asking them what I could possibly become with so little going for me. They assumed that with my grades (below sea level) I would amount to nothing, so my dad promised me that if I still hadn't landed a job at 35, he would buy me a small linen shop to run.

This is why, when I escaped to the UK, I pulled out the big guns and went straight into television. No one could stop me, because that fear of a linen shop was so strong. I didn't even need a script. I *was* the script, having rehearsed funny lines since my teens. From then on, I was off at the races, building up a persona like plates of armour around me.

I made up for the fact that I didn't fit in with any group by surrounding myself with people who seemingly liked me, mainly for being funny. It wasn't quite the same feeling as belonging, but it wasn't a bad stand-in for an isolated childhood.

I'm not saying you should feel sorry for me. Why should you, when I was the channeller of Joan Rivers? But it turns out that no matter how many people you're performing in front of, you might as well be in the middle of the Sahara because you have absolutely no feeling of connection with anyone. How can they connect when you're hiding behind some persona that's machine gunning them with schtick?

If you're not revealing the real you, why should they? And who is the real you anyway? You get so used to bending into shapes to make people like you, you forget to figure out where you are in all the gymnastics. Without insight, you never know what you need to be happy or to make others happy. So the gap between what you're putting out to feel less lonely, and what people are hearing, is dead space. Funny space, but dead space.

Before voicemail, I had an answering machine. I'd rush back to it at the end of the day to count how many beeps I received. My heart stopped as I counted those beeps. More than three and I was elated – less than three and I was heartbroken.

With social media, you'd think it was better because you could get faster feedback on how many people liked you in any particular moment. But social media is even more shallow than doing comedy because your audience's approval (or not) is based on whether your 280 characters are interesting enough. I'd sometimes sit up nights trying to make myself the *belle of the bon mot* in those 280 characters. Anything to squeeze out another follower to prove to myself that I mattered.

I think many of us spend lifetimes building up a tough front to show the world how well we're coping even when we're dying inside. It's such a waste of time because, in the end, no one really likes you for how impressive or accomplished you are. They may admire you and throw you a dinner party, make a speech about how much you've achieved, but they don't necessarily want to hang out with you. We all have a deep need to be seen and loved for who we are in our full-dimensional complexity. A little truth and vulnerability is the foundation of great relationships.

If two people are decked out in steel-plated, self-aggrandisement outfits, it can only be a you-scratch-my-back-

I'll-scratch-yours arrangement. People only feel safe with people who can come out from behind their armour so they know there's no hidden agenda. Maybe the opposite should be used as a new definition of love – amour without armour.

After my television career bombed, my fame went with it, and I could feel that old familiar loneliness rear its head.

Just before I learned about mindfulness, I used to indiscriminately grab people to be near me, so I didn't have to feel how lonely I was, using them like a bandage to wrap around my emptiness.

After practising mindfulness for a few years, I realised this was an old habit based on recordings from the past.

Those thoughts will try every trick in the book to get me back to believing them. Dragging up old memories from when I was ditched in the playground, when a boy didn't call me back, when a friend never spoke to me again, or when my heart was broken. The ammunition of past hurts never stops, but I've got some protection with grounding, breathing and kindness. Don't think I don't feel that loneliness most days, but I know it's just another habit, not a reality.

I've noticed, too, over the years, that when I'm with people with whom I can drop the mask, that loneliness disappears, along with feelings of shame, anger and fear (my usuals).

Ironically, I think you have to be alone to find this insight without distractions. In silence, if we don't panic or get swallowed by FOMO, we can find some peace.

There's a big difference between being alone and loneliness. If you're scared or empty inside, to be alone is hell. If you feel you're enough on your own and befriending your thoughts, aloneness becomes a pleasure. Not forever – we need people – but it's an option for a while, or at least a cheap holiday.

There are people who've been in forced isolation, in prison, who've found enlightenment. (My hero – Mandela.) It's usually when they're struggling against something or facing emotional turmoil (not when they're having a nice day) that people suddenly have an awakening and sometimes go on to change the world.

Exercise

Write down a list of situations where you felt the most lonely. Write a sentence or two to remind yourself what exactly made you feel that way.

Some situation examples:
★ at work
★ Christmas dinner
★ parties
★ on holiday
★ alone

Mine is at parties. I hate myself at parties.

Mindfulness exercise for loneliness

Sitting, standing or lying down.

G: Ground yourself by bringing focus to wherever you feel your body making contact with something solid (the floor or the chair). Now feel the breath entering through your nostrils or mouth, down into your lungs, your ribcage, and out again.

N: From your list above, bring in one of the situations where you felt lonely. Allow your mind to pull out memories, and now drop into your body to sense the feelings they bring up. Imagine exactly where they are: the edges, size and texture.

Now imagine on your inbreath that you're bringing in kindness (something like warmth or sunlight) to those areas and on your outbreath that you're letting out the toxins (dark smoke).

To finish, place your hand over your heart area and breathe into it and out again, so you feel the movement of your chest and your hand moving with each inhale and exhale.

S: Okay, now stop.

Exercise

Draw where the area of
loneliness was in your
body next to the outline.

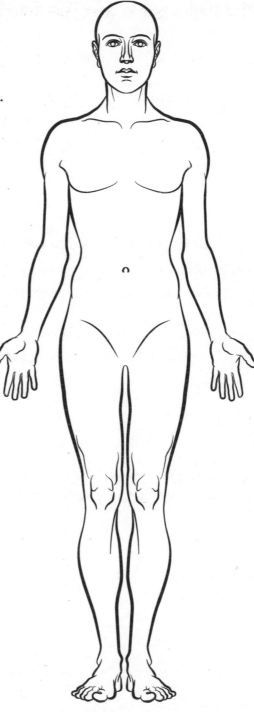

What did you picture when you brought in something good on your inbreath?

....

....

....

....

....

What did you picture when you brought in something negative on the outbreath?

....

....

....

....

....

How did you experience the sensation when your hand was over your heart – when you were breathing against your hand?

....

....

....

....

....

Reality check four: Change

We evolved to not acknowledge change. If we were constantly focused on the fact that everything ends and we all die, we wouldn't bother getting out of bed in the morning, let alone create civilisations. If we could be conscious that nothing is forever without getting depressed, we'd finally be able to embrace that thing we're all chasing, called "happiness".

We're good at acknowledging big changes. After all, we know we've been potty trained and have gone through puberty at some point. We've redecorated our houses, bought a new car, new shoes, birthed a kid, found a new partner or job and got older.

Our thoughts are about 1% of the 99% of stuff that's going on in our bodies. We're largely unaware of the other 99%, and there's no room to think about it in our measly 1% of thinking time.

Look at your arm. Now count to 10 and look again. Think it looks just the same? Think again.

While you were thinking about God-only-knows what else, trillions of cells died and were replaced by a trillion newborns without you realising it. Not only that, but we're completely unaware that our hair, nails and eyelashes are perpetually growing and falling out; that our digestive tract is filling up with and dumping waste; that our lungs are doing a covert deal with oxygen and carbon dioxide. So no, we don't notice change. A green healthy leaf isn't aware that at some point it's going to turn red, then fall to the ground and die. Same with us.

Humans have been blessed and cursed by not being made aware of change. The blessing is that we believe we'll wake up tomorrow pretty similar to how we are today. If we didn't, we'd go mad trying to remember where we put our socks.

Remember the guy in the film *Memento*? He couldn't remember a thing so he had to use himself as a Post-it note. That's how we'd end up too, tattooed from head to toe in shopping lists. Can you imagine looking down and learning from your inner thigh that you got married last week, and your elbow tells you that you had a child with the time and date of the birth? You'd be a mess. Luckily, we have a consistent story about ourselves, thanks to an autobiographical memory that stores big, important information about our likes, dislikes, our favourite food and who we're married to, but it's not tuned up to the subtle changes going on all the time.

Speaking of changes, the BBC decided after many years of silence to air all my interview shows and interview me in the studio to talk about them. I hadn't seen them for 25 years. For six days, eight hours a day, I had to sit there watching myself a quarter of a century younger. The first thing I did was scream, "Why didn't anyone tell me I was so cute?"

Of course, I'd been in make-up for several hours before filming each day, so that could have helped. But back then, I lived under the impression I was a dog. Now I realise I could have been having the time of my life. I actually was, but it would have been nice to do it with confidence. To be honest, I didn't recognise this person cracking jokes at 500 miles an hour, with a mouth so wide it covered the screen with wall-to-wall teeth, blocking all but the tiniest piece of a celebrity somewhere in the background.

The post-mindful me got to watch the pre-mindful me, and I saw all the old patterns I've been writing about in this workbook. Especially with the men (thanks Dad).

As I watched those shows, my rectum came out of my nose with horror. I went right back to my old habits of attacking with a smile on my face while being scared shitless. With Donald Trump, Bill Cosby, OJ and Don King. I kept trying to get their approval – why? And the more I tried to get them to appreciate me, the more they hated me. Even though I was ill after those interviews, filled with toxicity from the experience, I guess it still made good TV.

Before I completely diss myself, I have to say I was good with the girls and made some lasting friendships out of it. Fabulous, strong and hilarious women – Carrie Fisher, Bette Midler, Sharon Stone, Goldie Hawn and Pamela Anderson. What a gift.

Exercise: Keeping track of change

On the next page, you'll see a calendar with all the days of the month on it.

Choose 10 colours from your crayons and put them in the order of the mood they evoke. Decide which are the feel-good, positive colours and which are the feeling crap, negative colours, i.e. you decide yellow for positive is 1, green for less great is 4, maybe beige is neither positive or negative at 5. And then the colours get darker until black = 10.

At the end of a week or month, notice how your colours changed day by day. If they've stayed black for over a week, you've probably got depression.

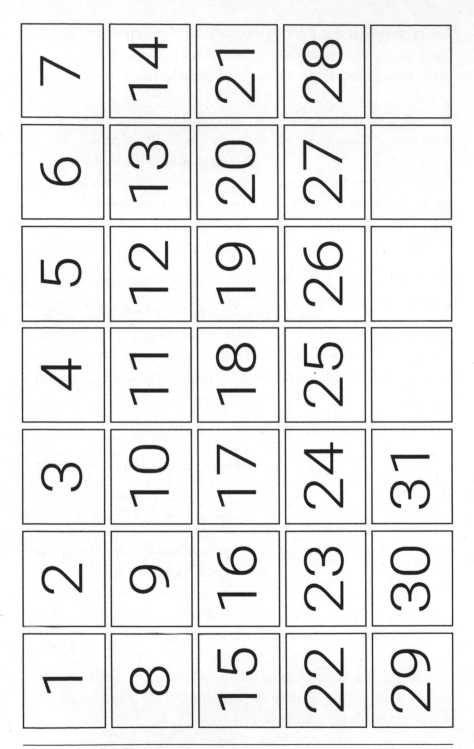

Mindfulness exercise one for noticing change

G: Sitting in a posture of wakefulness, your spine held erect but not rigid, aware of both of your feet on the floor and feeling the weight of your pelvis on the chair, grounded.

N: Notice the subtle details of your breathing, either in a small area (your nose, mouth, lungs, abdomen) or your whole torso.

When your thoughts enter, listen to them, but keep some of your focus on your body and breath. Trying to listen to them as if you're listening to a radio show might be easier.

R: Now escort your focus back to your breath.

S: Okay, now stop.

Exercise

Write down five thoughts you remember or your general mood.

Besides these, write down from 1 to 10 how disturbing you found them – 1 is not at all, 10 is upsetting.

1 ....

....

2 ....

....

3 ....

....

4 ....

....

5 ....

....

Now go back to doing mindfulness.

Mindfulness exercise two for noticing change

G: Grounding your feet on the ground, your bum on the chair.

N: Now send your focus to the sense of your hands and become aware of where they contact your lap or each other. Send your awareness to notice if they're clamped, relaxed, hot or cold.

Now, widening your lens, bring your focus to your breathing through your whole torso. You might want to open up your awareness to take in sounds, letting them come to you without having to hunt for them.

So now you're aware of it all: feet on the ground, bum on the chair, hands in your lap. At a certain point, inviting the thoughts to come in. Keeping most of your focus on your body breathing, tune into what your thoughts are.

R: Before finishing, let go of the thoughts and come back to your breathing.

S: Okay, now stop.

Exercise

Again, during this second exercise write down five phrases you remember, or your general mood. Besides these, write down from 1 to 10 how disturbing you found them – 1 is not at all, 10 is upsetting.

1 ....

....

2 ....

....

3 ....

....

4 ....

....

5 ....

....

Take a look at both exercises and note how dramatically your thoughts change without you having to do anything. They have their own agenda.

Jon Kabat-Zinn Lake Mindfulness

Mindfulness – healing lake
(This is a Jon Kabat-Zinn meditation.)

Lying on a bed, sofa or on the floor, get as comfortable as you can.

Allowing your eyes to close and the sense of your body to melt into whatever you're lying on.

When you feel ready, picture the image of a lake, maybe one you know or one you imagine. Picture how it's held in the earth. Notice how the lake is always changing. Sometimes it's calm and smooth as glass, reflecting everything around it: the sky, trees, sun. Sometimes it's like a mirror, sometimes there are turbulent waves crashing into each other.

Imagine your body is this lake held by the earth, reflecting the changing of your thoughts, bodily sensations, impulses and sounds. But even when your mind is choppy or wild, you can drop down below the surface and watch the changes above you. So rather than get caught up in the tempestuous conditions reflecting your thoughts, you have the option to sink to the bottom of the lake and observe the changes from down there from a point of stillness. So whatever's going on up on the surface, you're just lying or sitting on the sandy floor, at one with the fish.

Exercise: Pre-planning for change

We know nothing stays the same and you can't be sure of anything, so why not make a list of things for when the change comes, so you're ready with a plan. Think of these suggestions to yourself as though you're packing a parachute.

Here are some plans I made in the past that helped when the carpet was pulled out from under me.

My biggest fear was losing my job in television. Knowing that very few women survive a career in television in their 50s, I had a gut feeling that my time was running out and I was about to be dumped. So just before my 50th birthday, I applied to psychotherapy school so that when I was eventually dumped, even though I knew I'd be devastated, at least I'd be ready.

I always dreaded my kids leaving home. When my eldest son left for university, I wailed like an animal, clutching his suitcase, my nails embedded in his ankles as he dragged me down the road. I vowed to never let this happen again. Before my daughters could leave me for university, I enrolled myself into Oxford and went away before they did.

Write down your plans for the "just in case" situation.

1 ....

....

....

....

....

....

2 ....

....

....

....

....

3 ....

....

....

....

....

4 ....

....

....

....

....

5 ....

....

....

....

....

Reality check five: Dissatisfaction

Problem solvers

At a certain point in evolution, about 150,000 years ago, our brain had a growth spurt and grew three times its size. It made enough synaptic connections (which make the brain bigger) to bring on language.

When language came along, so did thinking – and just in time too, otherwise there would be no civilisation, art, literature, science, architecture or technology. You name it, thinking was behind it.

Once thinking was possible, it became part of our repertoire. So much so, that if you throw us a problem, we will answer it, even if we have to be persecuted in its pursuit. See Galileo, Socrates, Jesus and everyone else who got the chop for coming up with original answers to unresolved questions, e.g. is the earth flat? Did God have a son? And if he did, who was he?

This problem solving has been our modus operandi since we began, and it worked like a dream when it came to things like defending ourselves. We were brilliant at everything, from whittling spears to building missiles.

Communication was also a natural-born gift. We went from shouting into cans connected by string to building an iPhone 12 (there may be more versions by the time this book comes out).

Before thinking came along, we worked off animal instincts. If something large with teeth was around and ran fast, we knew to run like hell in the opposite direction. If something small was scuttling around, we knew it was dinner. Language, though, gave us not only the ability to think, but to think to ourselves (self-talk). Both abilities are activated in the same regions in the brain. So now we could really go for it on the problem-solving front.

Bad news about problem solving

Basically, our problem-solving technique is to face a problem and seek an answer. Between those two states is a gap. The problem with problem solving is that we humans give most of our energy to closing that gap. Some gaps can't be closed, and the wider the chasm from problem to answer, the more dissatisfied and unhappy we become. This same skill that helped us build civilisation is also the source of our anguish.

When we come up with an emotional problem like "Why aren't I happy?", our brains will churn forever to solve it, relentlessly digging up the past, which may bring up unhappy memories. Those unhappy memories simply add to the question of why we're not happy, and the gap gets bigger.

Our brains store more negative memories than positive memories. (We're Velcro for negative thoughts and Teflon for positive ones.) Again, for survival reasons, it's better to remember mistakes so as not to make the same ones again when facing a dangerous situation.

We can't solve emotional problems with cognitive thinking. That kind of thinking is useful when building the pyramids or figuring out bank statements. But "Why aren't I happy?" isn't going to work, because if you try to close the gap of wanting to be happy and figuring out why you aren't, you'll probably open the door to those critical thoughts, "Something must be wrong with me." "Maybe I don't deserve to be happy?" "No one likes me."

People sometimes think if they worry enough, they'll come up with a conclusion. This type of thinking will only lead to an ulcer or acid reflux and a closet full of Pepto Bismol (I have cases – call me).

Why we're not happy

We live at a time where people are looking for happiness in all the wrong places, mainly because we're not quite sure what we're after. Is it that buzzy, sugar rush of happiness mainlined straight into the heart that everyone's after, or something else?

Whatever that something else is, it's not advertised on Google or available on Amazon. Advertisers know how to keep us shopping by setting out bespoke bait for our individual addictions and knowing exactly when to yank us in for the kill. They prey like vultures on our dissatisfaction, promising we'll be happy if we buy this shoe, this car, this patio set. Of course, we never will be because someone's always got a better shoe, car and patio set. (They've got me addicted to Netflix. I've worn my fingerprint away to nothing from hitting the "next episode" tab.)

We're constantly reminded, at every turn, how many people are liked, followed or watched far more than we are. Comparison is the current gazumper of happiness. This leaves us with a feeling that we are lacking and that the next person is having a better life. Probably they're feeling it about the next person, and so on and so forth, like a dysfunctional domino effect.

We're brainwashed into thinking the craving will stop if we get enough stuff. But it's this constant hunger for more that depletes us. We're in a culture of emotional starvation.

We're at the beck and call of dopamine, a chemical we produce in ourselves. This is great for motivating us to seek a certain amount of success, reward or accomplishment. (You don't win a gold without some "oomph" in your tank.) But if we're pumping dopamine simply to get a buzz out of conquering something, it will only lead to disappointment. It won't be long before we'll need to conquer something else. What's more, the buzz doesn't actually come from the getting of something, it comes from the hunt or chase. As soon as the prize is in our hands, the fun stops and the dopamine drops.

After a while, as with all addictions, it doesn't even get us high any more – it just gets us feeling normal. So we dream of a day when the hit is so big the craving stops. "When I win the lottery." "When I finally retire." "When I finally meet the perfect partner." It's never going to happen.

We humans have a homeostatic baseline, so however excited we get, we always return to it. They say after you have more than £65,000 pounds, the thrill doesn't increase with the increase of money. It comes back to baseline. I think it picks up again after a few million. They say after about five years of being passionately in love, you go back to your baseline of feelings about the other person – not too excited and not asleep (if it doesn't nosedive first).

Those who retire have been known to sink into a sofa of sadness and never get up again.

We're on the hunt for happiness to fill our emptiness. The buzz won't fill it, it will only ignite the sense of purposelessness and lead to more seeking.

Dissatisfaction exercise

Write down:

what you want and can't have

....

....

....

....

....

....

....

....

....

what you have and don't want

....
....
....
....
....
....

what you think would make you happy

....
....
....
....
....
....

why you ultimately know it won't make you happy

....
....
....
....
....
....

Reality check six:
Death

Your instinct may tell you to not read this. Most people don't want to know about death. But, as with all the other realities, if you don't look, sooner or later they'll jump out of the box and surprise you.

The point of this book is to get ready, so now I'm getting you ready for death. You'll thank me in the end. We need to remember that life is a temp job, not a permanent one. If you can deal with death and the fear of death, then facing the other five realities is a breeze.

Death encompasses:

★ **Difficult emotions.** Some people may be at peace at their end, but I would say chances are huge that most of us might feel panic, fear, hysteria, anger, despair, sadness...

★ **Uncertainty.** Who knows when it's showing up but you'll know when it does.

★ **Loneliness.** No matter how many friends or family you have, when it comes to the very end, you're on your own.

★ **Change.** This is your last change. And it's a big one. There's nothing else coming unless you believe in the afterlife, then you better have a clean pair of pants nearby (see Egyptian Pharaohs).

★ **Dissatisfaction.** No one is thrilled about dying, yet we know it's out there somewhere. This is why there's a whirring of unhappiness playing in the background throughout our lives. Even when you're on holiday, it's whirring away.

★ **Death.** As Sting sort of sings (I changed the lyrics slightly):
"Every breath you take, every move you make, every step
you take, death is watching you...."

This sound went from whirring to blaring during Covid,
because death was evident everywhere. We shook with terror
in our homes, wondering if we were going to catch it. And we
shook for our friends and family, especially the older ones.

Who was next? That's what was always on our minds, thanks to
the relentless death toll every night on the news. I think they
should open *Newsnight* with a few bars from "Bring out the
dead" accompanied with a bell.

Even though millions have been Covid vaccine-jabbed, people
still can't get enough. Just now, I'm sitting in a park writing
this, and someone near me has a radio on top volume reporting
when the next waves of Covid are hitting other countries
because it's dropped so low in the UK. A little good news, and
we're immediately looking elsewhere to find our fear.

When you don't have to think about death and when you do

We can get away with not thinking about it until about the
age of 30, even though accidents can happen. From about
50 onwards, thoughts of our termination accelerate with its
accompanying signs of aging, which no one ever warns you
about – nose hairs, crinkling of thighs, ever-enlarging breasts
and, for men, a pregnant stomach.

Woody Allen famously said, "It's not that I'm afraid of dying, it's just that I don't want to be there when it happens."

Even Aristotle made a joke about it. He said, "Luck is when the guy next to you gets hit with an arrow."

Ernest Becker didn't write funny lines. He was an American cultural anthropologist and author of the 1974 Pulitzer Prize-winning book *The Denial of Death* (not a humour book) but he still gives a great quote:

"This is the paradox. A human is out of nature and hopelessly in it. We are dual: Up in the stars and yet housed in a heart-pumping, breath-gasping body that once belonged to a fish and still carries the gill marks to prove it. A human is literally split in two. We have an awareness of our own splendid uniqueness in that we stick out of nature with a towering majesty, and yet we go back into the ground a few feet in order to blindly and dumbly rot and disappear forever. It is a terrifying dilemma to be in and to have to live with."

He says humans naturally feel anxious and helpless in a world where they know they're fated to die. We spend our entire lives building an illusory, unchangeable solid identity known as "self". We build structures of security around it, i.e. a steady job, accomplishments, having a lot of friends, all to help us create the illusion that because we have so much going for us, we're invincible.

Don't we know by now that death really doesn't care what you do for a living or how much money you make? We've become obsessed with doing things we'd like to be remembered for, but don't acknowledge that for that to happen, we have to die first.

At this very moment, I'm compulsively finishing writing this workbook. I'm on the final reality now – death, which might just happen to me as I haven't slept for a week.

I tend to get overly focused on things, not only because I'm a workaholic and seek infinite approval, but I know deep down that I'm doing all this to avoid thinking about my death. I'm not kidding – that's how I think and always have.

Another one of my almost daily thoughts is that I'll be much older when I finish this book than when I started it. At this point, I don't even have to think about death, I'm writing about it. What I really don't like to think about is aging but I do – constantly. When I look in a mirror, I assume it's someone else who needs a lot of work done. Should I tell her?

I can't even say what age I am out loud. The actual number just stops at my lips and won't come out. I've always had a fear of aging. At 29, I thought by 30 it would be all over for me – I would be alone and miserable for the rest of my life. Then I thought it would be all over by 40. At 50, I was so mortified, I tried to scratch out my date of birth in my passport.

I never told anyone how old I was. I only told Ed (my husband) as we were walking down the aisle, alongside the fact that I had mental illness. It was too late for him to run, so he got stuck with a woman much older than him who was crazy to boot. Marina, my daughter, has been brainwashed that I'm 32. People look at her with pity when she tells them.

I found some writings of mine from when I was in my 30s and realised I was thinking about death even back then. I also had depression back then, so it makes sense. I wrote:

"There are moments in your life, where you're slapped in the face with the bigger picture. As if the universe is saying to you, 'Can you take this? Can you live knowing you're going to die?' That someday that curtain of delusion will be ripped away and suddenly you'll be face to face with your own insignificance? You realise you're here on earth for a millisecond and then blown away by the howling winds of time.

"At one point you're a child, wishing you were older, and you can't wait for Christmas to come. And then Christmas comes and goes and suddenly you're a teenager; a rebel smoking cigarettes, with long hair and a coat made of goat, and you think this is forever. And just as you get used to it, you're an adult and you get an adult job and people invite you to dinner parties and expect you to make sense and not pop balloons in their faces. And before you can adjust your dials, you're a mother, and then you realise, this just keeps going on ... This can't stop ... And then you get older, and then, in the end, there's nothingness, emptiness, a void."

I also found this, which I must have written in my 40s:

"When you're a kid, you have no fear about trying anything. I mean we're born with limitless possibilities. I had a friend who wanted to be a fireman with absolutely no question of qualifications. I wanted to be a mermaid. When you're young, everything is possible. You look at a snowflake for hours and watch cloud patterns. Everything is novel, in full living technicolor and you're excited out of your mind. Then you get older and some fucker tells you you can't be a mermaid for whatever reason. As you get older still, your world gets tinier and tinier because you believe you don't have options until one day you end up in a rut.

"And no one seems to mind that we end up using such a tiny part of our potential; we just think, 'Oh well, this is how I ended up.' When we talk about old people, we say things like, 'Oh that's just how Tootles is – when you get old, they give you names of pets – she does the same thing every day; she has her tea at 4 and then biccies at 6, then sleepies at 7.' And we think that's wonderful that she's got a routine.

"What's really happening is that we get caught in behavioural habits, and that's how we slowly lose our minds. When your brain learns new things or you experience new things, your neurons grow branches. And the denser the forest, the more versatile and alive you are. If you stop learning or experiencing things, the branches wither away and you end up on a sofa watching reruns of CNN. You want not to be dead when you're still actually alive.

"Break your old habits, change chairs, change friends, learn the tango, parachute out of a plane. You're old, what's the worst that could happen? And no matter how much you have to let go of in the end, if you can notice things as if for the first time, notice their novelty, it will outweigh how much stuff you've accumulated or what job you had. And then you could still end up a mermaid."

Anyway, as I've said, no one is allowed to say my age (even if they somehow know it) at the risk of a beheading or cancellation of all future Christmas presents. People tell me I should be proud at this point of how much I've accomplished. I should be able to look back at my career and go, "Wow!" But I can't.

I think I inherited this from my mother who never told anyone her age. I had to make it up when she died. I once took her to a doctor when she was already gaga. When the doctor asked her how old she was, she retorted proudly, "Fifty-two, though I may be off by a few years." She then took out her pen and tried to smoke it. (She forgot she had given up smoking cigarettes years ago.)

My now-deceased mother and I aren't the only ones who fear death and aging. (In her case she's not scared anymore – she's dead, so all that worry didn't get her anywhere.) Biohackers in Silicon Valley are stuffing themselves with supplements, getting blood from young people for blood transfusions to live longer or putting their brains and/or bodies in liquid nitrogen, doing cryopreservation so they can make another appearance some day in the future. Like coming out for an encore.

But how do those of us who aren't insane deal with death? I researched this, and found out that when some people were told they had a limited time to live, they began to appreciate every moment and became much more present. I would think most people would be hitting the heroin, but they said they felt more alive than they ever did before.

The Buddhists (who I've praised earlier and will again at the end of this book) thought about how to deal with impermanence 2,500 years ago. They were so ahead of the game. Impermanence is at the very heart of Buddhist teachings. In a strange way, impermanence works for us, in that when you're feeling any of the Big Six realities and you realise they're impermanent too, it makes them easier to bear.

The Buddhists believe we should put the scarcity of time at the front and centre of our consciousness; to wake up to the fact that this show is not going on forever. Wake up to the fact that one day we won't wake up. That this life is a party on death row. They believe we should be okay with it.

The benefit of facing death is that you're not wasting your time and energy trying to block it out, so you have more energy for living. What you value becomes crystal clear; you stop wasting time with people who are draining you, doing things because someone talked you into it, and taking on more work because it keeps you busy. You won't be distracted by superficial things because you haven't got time. Now you've got all the insight you could ever desire.

This Buddhist mindfulness exercise below might bring up feelings of anxiety, fear and panic in some people.

Remember what we did with the difficult emotions body scan? When we experience those feelings as a raw body sensation, stories about how terrible it was or how much we didn't want to feel them, we need to let them drop away so they lose their intensity.

Awareness lets us hold emotions as a sensation without triggering the painful thoughts, judgments or interpretations that usually accompany them. We're uncoupling the senses from the thoughts. So when you say the sentences below, be aware of the feelings and then imagine wrapping them in kindness by breathing into them.

Mindfulness exercise for facing impermanence
(written by a Buddhist teacher)

Say these lines to yourself once a day:

> Just like everyone, I am of the nature to age. I have not gone beyond aging.
>
> Just like everyone, I am of the nature to sicken. I have not gone beyond sickness.
>
> Just like everyone, I am of the nature to die. I have not gone beyond dying.
>
> Just like everyone, all that is mine, beloved and pleasing, will change, will become otherwise, will become separated from me.

Here is an outline of a body. Draw in where you felt any reactions to the above lines.

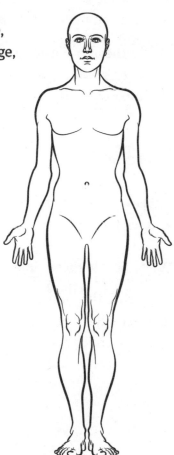

Write down what the sensations felt like. Tingling? Stabbing? Numbness?

....

....

....

....

....

....

....

I hope the above exercise wasn't too disturbing. If you're feeling brave, let's face some more impermanence together by trying this next exercise.

Exercise

This exercise is to help you decide what's important in your life and what isn't.

Write beside these times what you'd do if you had that amount of time left to live?

one hour

....

....

....

....

one day

....

....

....

one week

....

....

....

six months

....

....

....

five years

....

....

....

a lifetime

....

....

....

Write down if an idea came up for every time period.

Write down if there's something you might do now in your life, based on what you wrote down.

Exercise on regret

This following exercise is based on research looking into what people on their deathbed most regretted not having done in their lives. Their regrets were:

★ I wish I had gotten divorced earlier.
★ I wish I had taken a job for the love of the work, not the money.
★ I wish I had played and enjoyed myself more.

This exercise allows us to reassess our priorities and change things now, while we still can.

Write down three things you'd still like to do and would regret if you didn't do them.

1 ....

....

....

....

2 ....

....

....

....

3 ....

....

....

....

Mindfulness meditation for death – using your breath

Lying down on a bed or sofa.

G: Ground yourself by feeling every point of contact between your body and the surface; your heels, back of legs, pelvis, torso, arms and back of your head.

N: Now send focus to your body as a whole and become aware of your breath filling it and leaving it. Feel your skin expanding and contracting as you feel yourself melting into the bed. As you lie there, imagine that each breath is your last one.

R: When the thoughts come (and, boy, will they, with this exercise) gently refocus back to the sense of your body breathing. Imagine each inhale is your last and each exhale is your last, filling your body with kindness and compassion. So, even though you're imagining that this could be your last breath, you're still soothing yourself as a counterbalance to keep you emotionally steady doing this difficult exercise.

S: Okay, now stop. (Not stop as in dying, just stop the exercise.)

Write down:

how the image of the last breath made you feel

....

....

....

how the self-soothing made you feel

....

....

....

You can use the above exercise with almost any activity:

walking (imagine it's your last walk)

....

....

....

eating (imagine it's your last meal)

....

....

....

reading (imagine it's your last book)

....

....

....

Write your own activities to apply the exercise to, and write down your reactions afterwards.

Okay, that's it from me. And here's someone who can say it much better.

Thich Nhat Hanh says, "Life is impermanent, but that does not mean that it is not worth living. It is precisely because of its impermanence that we value life so dearly. Therefore we must know how to live each moment deeply and use it in a responsible way. If we are able to live the present moment completely, we will not feel regret later. We will know how to care for those who are close to us and how to bring them happiness.

Perhaps less accumulation of things; perhaps less of an obsession with unattainable security; perhaps less of a preoccupation with 'becoming someone', not so much living for the 'future', because there isn't one. Is it possible to have fulfillment in this moment? To learn how to die is also to learn how to live. Death can serve as a 'coach', encouraging us to live completely in the present, with more confidence and less fear."

Buddhism

I'm not a Buddhist. Okay, I have one of those ting ting bowls, but I only use it for special occasions and have never done it in front of anyone (I'm a closet tinger). Even though I'm not a Buddhist, I've stolen most of their ideas and translated them into "my speak" for this workbook. I'm sure they don't mind – after all, they're so giving.

Earlier in my life, I avoided learning about Buddhism because I don't have enough breath to get to the end of a word like *Dhammacakkappavattana*. I thought it was a misprint and the computer had gone crazy, but it turns out to be the first discourse of Buddha after his enlightenment. You would think that if you're enlightened, you could make a shorter word, but no, the discourse is called *Dhammacakkappavattana Sutta*. This means "Noble Truths", and then I read that "Noble Truths" isn't really an accurate description. Well, if it's not accurate, why did they come up with it? Life is too short.

Though it's not a formal religion, they say the *dharma* (an unbelievably short word describing the concepts behind the nature of the human mind – why we suffer and our potential for happiness) was communicated by Buddha in what was called the Four Noble Truths.

The First Noble Truth is the fundamental problem of life known as *dukkha*. No one agrees what it really means. Some say it means suffering, others say it's a disease of the human condition, others say it's unease. Whatever it is, it should be avoided at all costs. It gets worse – the Pali word for the wider meaning of *dukkha* is *duhkhaduhkha*.

Whhhhhhhaaaaattttt?

We're destined to suffer because of the existence of the Big Six, and there's nothing we can do about this unless we free ourselves by training our minds.

The Second Noble Truth is all about the causes of pain or *dukkha* (now it means pain). We suffer because, even if we have happiness, it's impermanent and everything changes. (What have I been saying in this book?) The causes of suffering are ceaseless craving, clinging and attachment to things that won't last. The nature of craving is written in the *Dhammacakkappavuttana Sutta* - read it.

This craving leads to attachments. You may have an attachment to objects (new car) or an attachment to views (I hate Republicans) or an attachment to the idea of self (I don't like broccoli). All attachments and craving lead to suffering, and all suffering comes from craving and attachments. (He couldn't say it enough.) But he delivered some good news that craving can be eradicated. Buddha didn't believe you could stop this craving through abdication, flagellation or starvation, but you could change your relationship to craving through the practice of mindfulness. It allows you to see things how they really are, not what your thoughts tell you they are.

The Third Noble Truth is how to burn off the effects of greed, delusion and aversion. Learning how to stop craving is by investigating the nature of the mind – mindfulness.

And the Fourth Noble Truth is how to practise mindfulness, which has been presented to you compliments of this workbook: *A Mindfulness Guide for Survival.*

And there we have it, Buddha and I both on the same page.

I'd like to end by telling you what I did today – the day this workbook was due. I have been up for a week, day and night trying to hit the deadline. This morning, I was so burnt out, I decided to get in the car and go swimming with my daughter in the canal in Horley.

I spent about 20 minutes swimming, happy to be alive. We then sat down to do mindfulness together, and I happened to call my publisher, asking her why I needed to hand the workbook in today and could I have one more day.

She said, "No."

And I lost it.

I had an earpiece hanging out of my ear, with a recording of Tara Brach telling me to "Let go of my thoughts and be calm", as I stood up, soaking wet in my swimsuit, weeping in anger and howling. All this was coming from a woman who had just written a book on mindfulness. I was aware how crazy this was seconds after I hung up.

What can I say? We are all works in progress.

In the past, I would, by now, have slid into one of my deeper depressions, which always followed that kind of high-octane outburst. The good news is I haven't. Of course I'm hoping my publisher will forgive me. I mean *I'm* trying to forgive me.

But my point is that even with practising mindfulness, if the conditions are bad (no sleep, lots of stress and triggers), we (I) can all fall right back into the hole we've (I've) been digging ourselves out of for years. Mindfulness is just something we (I) have to keep exercising. Hopefully, someday I'll catch my quick temper before I even open my mouth. But, as I said, till then I too remain a work in progress.

After I got home, I was thinking about death as I finally wrapped up this book. As I pressed the "send" button, I decided what I'd like on my epitaph.

I just want it to read: "She tried."

Afterthought

Even though this book nearly frazzled me to a cinder (I had three months to write it), what I learned from the research and following the exercises, was life-changing. I've been doing mindfulness regularly for years and yet there's still such a gap in between what I practise and the unhealthy habits I haven't been able to break – at least, so far. It's changed me in positive ways - I've largely managed to ween myself off my addiction to rage. I'm less frazzled, more present these days, but the act of self-compassion is still something I find difficult, especially when I feel I've failed. I'm still a cruel slave-driver to myself. I suppose it comes from taking over the whip from my parents. It's less than in the past, but still harsh.

The insight I've gained from writing this book was finding out what was behind some of my past behaviours: constantly pushing for attention, pushing to be liked and pushing to succeed. I assumed all this was the result of unleashed ambition, low self-esteem and pushy parents. It wasn't. Those traits came out of a deep fear of the Big Realities I've been writing about. Some are a breeze; I can deal with change (actually I thrive on it), and uncertainty is my middle name, but my dread of loneliness, dissatisfaction and my real biggie, death, was so deeply buried, I didn't know they were even there.

I handed in the book last week, teeth chattering, shoulders rigid with tension, brain burnt after five all-nighters to hit the deadline. Tomorrow I'm going to a silent mindfulness retreat called "breath and death" for 12 days. I was so inspired by the research on death – (in the last chapter) – how life-enhancing it can be when you accept it, how each moment becomes more vivid and meaningful when you know there's an end, that I signed up for the retreat as soon as I heard about it. My books give me an excuse to let my curiosity run riot and each one has always led me to my next adventure. I'm dedicated to re-invention and always wanting to be surprised; that's what I live for. I'll let you know how the death retreat goes – probably in my next book. Okay, not probably... definitely.

Bibliography

Antonio Damasio: *The Feeling of What Happens: Body, Emotion and the Making of Consciousness*

Giovanni Frazzetto: *How We Feel: What science can – and can't – tell us about our emotions*

Rupert Gethin: *The Foundations of Buddhism*

Daniel Goleman and Dalai Lama XIV: *Destructive Emotions and How We Can Overcome Them*

Jon Kabat-Zinn: *Coming to Our Senses: Healing Ourselves and the World Through Mindfulness*

Candace. B. Pert PH.D.: *Molecules of Emotions: Why You Feel the Way You Feel*

Gelong Thubten: *A Monk's Guide to Happiness: Meditation in the 21st Century*

Eckhart Tolle: *A New Earth: Awakening Your Life's Purpose*

Mark Williams: *Mindfulness: A practical guide to finding peace in a frantic world*

Notes